11·22·77

FAITH
OF OUR
FATHERS

VOLUME FOUR

Religion, Awakening and Revolution

Martin E. Marty

A Consortium Book

Library of Congress Card Catalog Number: 77-9558
ISBN: 0-8434-0623-2
ISBN: 0-8434-0636-4 paper

ACKNOWLEDGEMENTS

From THE FORMING OF AN AMERICAN TRADITION by Leonard J. Trinterud. Copyright MCMXLIX, by W.L. Jenkins, The Westminster Press. Used by permission.

William H. Nelson, THE AMERICAN TORY, c Oxford University Press 1961.
By permission of the Oxford University Press.

To
John Henry Gienapp
Teacher of Writing
"Name not writ in water..."

Preface

This book was written during my term as an Associate Dean at The University of Chicago Divinity School. I wish to thank Dean Joseph M. Kitagawa for the help and encouragement he provided and to Assistant to the Dean Delores Smith for making arrangements for the production of this manuscript. Two other members of our decanal team in Swift Hall 101, Cheryl Paymaster and Diane McLaughlin deserve generous thanks for their patient and successful efforts to decipher my handwritten corrections and to transcribe my roughly typed drafts in preparation for publication. As always, students in my history classes and seminars made more contributions than they will here recognize.

Much of the material in *Religion, Awakening and Revolution* was delivered as The Lowell Lectures at Boston University School of Theology and as the Sprunt Lectures at Union Theological Seminary in Richmond, Virginia in 1975-76.

Martin E. Marty
The University of Chicago
May 1, 1977

Table of Contents

PART THREE: THE REVOLUTION

It seems no unnatural conclusion from ancient prophecy, ... that in order to usher in...the *latter-day-glory*, TWO GREAT REVOLUTIONS are to take place; the *first* outward and political; the *second* inward and spiritual.

David Austin, 1794

PART ONE

The Lack of Intentions

1

The Apparent Bystanders

Utmost Good Faith Towards the Indians

In 1700 an Indian skull remained on display where it had been for twenty-four years, atop a pole in the Pilgrims' town of Plymouth, Massachusetts. It had belonged to the Wampanoag chief named King Philip who, in alliance with the Narragansetts, struck at the whites. The Indians resented the Puritans, who had, among other things, wanted them to keep the Christian Sabbath and to be punished for blasphemies against the whites' God. The ensuing war was devastating to both sides. Over a thousand New Englanders were killed. The survivors who won celebrated God's victory by butchering Philip and mounting his skull as a grisly image of vengeance.

The eighteenth century whites' images of the American Indians, whose roots on this continent antedated their own by perhaps 30,000 years, were not always so stark as the skull. Two years into the century there appeared the most extensive written history of American religion to date, Cotton Mather's provincial and presumptuous *Magnalia Christi Americana*. The Harvard-bred pedant who pastored Boston's Second Church wanted his work to have a continental scope. He began his epic:

I WRITE the WONDERS of the CHRISTIAN RELIGION, flying from the depravations of *Europe*, to the

3

American Strand; And, assisted by the Holy Author of
that *Religion,* I do.... Report the *Wonderful Displays* of
His infinite Power, Wisdom, Goodness, and Faithful-
ness, wherewith His Divine Providence hath *Irradiated*
an *Indian Wilderness.*

Mather wrote at a time when some whites still had a taste
for converting Indians. He proudly noted that the great seal
of the Massachusetts Bay Colony portrayed *"a poor Indian
having a label going from his mouth with a* COME OVER
AND HELP US." The reference was to a biblical moment
when the Gospel had passed from Asia to Europe as now it
was passing from Europe to America. A Macedonian then
had come to the apostle Paul in a vision with a label going
from *his* mouth, "Come over and help us."

Cotton Mather, who descended from two distinguished
lines of pioneer preachers, the Cottons and the Mathers,
always remembered that a motive of the original colonists
had been to come over to help the natives. He recalled that
the great missionary John Eliot had been

awakened by those expressions in the royal charter, in
the assurance and protection whereof this wilderness
was first peopled; namely, 'To win and incite the natives
of that country to the knowledge and obedience of the
only true God and Saviour of mankind, and the Christian
faith, is our royal intention, and the adventurer's free
profession is the principal end of the plantation.

That was long ago. The eighteenth century planters were
not forgetting the plans of their fathers and mothers. Mather
himself, according to his diaries of later years, kept writing
for Indians, appealing for funds to help them, serving on
boards and bureaus on their behalf, and helping support
schools for them. In 1725 he still cared for the "dying
Religion among those miserable objects." But his major book
revealed that in the front of his mind was the supplanting of
the faiths of the Indians' fathers and the growth of an
American Israel. He still noticed Indian origins, practices,

and vices and hinted that now and then some whites were on familiar terms with natives. He showed that there was still some care for non-church-members, some recall of duty to promote welfare to Indians.

Mather was more concerned, however, simply to explain the Indians' presence and their past. God had "brought a vine out of *England*" to "cast out the heathen" so that there could be "room for a *better growth*," for the *"chosen generation."* The Indians, therefore, were also pernicious creatures, diabolical hypocritical wretches, Scythian wolves, inaccessible enemies, likeness to devils, *"salvage hounds"* who worried God's "dear *flocks."* It would be *"the most unexceptionable piece of justice to extinguish them."*

In the year 1739 one greater than Mather, Jonathan Edwards, preached thirty sermons that were to provide the core for his *History of the Work of Redemption.* This "great work," which was to be "a body of divinity in an entirely new method, being thrown into the form of a history" was never finished. But the sermonic notes provided him a chance for one more reflection on the meaning of the faith of Indian fathers. The ordinarily humane man who spent seven years ministering to Housatonic Indians at Stockbridge explained Indian existence in terms that differed little from the standard view:

Here the many nations of Indians worshipped [Satan] as God from age to age, while the gospel was confined to the opposite side of the globe. It is probably supposed, from some remaining accounts, that the occasion of first peopling America was this: that the devil, being alarmed and surprised by the wonderful success of the gospel the first three hundred years after Christ, and by the downfall of the Heathen empire in the time of Constantine - and seeing the gospel spread so fast, and fearing that his Heathenish kingdom would be wholly overthrown through the world—led away a people from the other continent into America, that they might be quite out of the reach of the gospel, that here he might quietly possess them, and reign over them as their god...

People who think in these terms might very well carry on a mission to Indians. The Puritans did in the beginning, but their readiness for such work lessened with each battle against them. By the end of the colonial era only a handful of missionaries still worked among the tribes in New England. Those who saw Indians as Satan's people would not be likely to try to appreciate the faith of Indians' fathers. If before century's end these whites were to be joining in a revolution that proclaimed liberty, equality, and justice for all, such a revolution had to be unintended—or else Indians could not be considered part of the 'all'. Appreciation of world religions was part of the concurrent European Enlightenment; "the greatest revolution in the European mind since Christianity had overwhelmed paganism," according to historian Peter Gay, but Jonathan Edwards, the finest mind in America, only "serenely affirmed the faith of his fathers," and could not positively appraise that of Indians.

More than two centuries later white-Indian understandings have improved so little and positive grasps of other faiths have developed so slightly that few Christian heirs of the Mather or the Edwards clans are in position to judge the patriarchs for their judgments and bewilderments. Perhaps two thirds of a million of these natives—about the same number as today!—originally stood between the Christians and their new Israel, their empire. The newcomers were planters who did not know what to make of a hunting culture, literates who disdained illiteracy, people of order bewildered over the varieties of Indian religious experience and culture. They had a dim sense of the Indians' respect for nature and tribe. But they saw what later might be seen as the 'animism' of many Indian expressions to be what the Bible called idolatry. The Indians must be Christianized, removed, or extinguished. Revolutionary thoughts of equality and freedom were remote; humane instincts were the best to be hoped for.

Now and then people of the eighteenth century religious world left behind traces of such humane appreciations. Charming and naive is the account of a Moravian missionary in Pennsylvania, the Reverend John Heckewelder, who reports on a mild encounter he had with travelling Indians in 1777 at Gnadenhutten. The issue there as almost always was one of space: who owned and who might best use the land? The Indians had put their horses over night to pasture in his little meadow.

I called on them in the morning to learn why they had done so. I endeavoured to make them sensible of the injury they had done me...One of them replied: My friend, it seems you lay claim to the grass my horses have eaten, because you had enclosed it with a fence: now tell me, who caused the grass to grow? Can *you* make the grass grow? I think not, and no body can except the great Mannitto. He it is who causes it to grow for my horses and for yours! See, friend! the grass which grows out of the earth is common to all; the game in the woods is common to all....If you will consider, you will find that my horses did not eat *all* your grass. For friendship's sake, however, I shall never put my horses in your meadow again.

After such an exchange, there is no wonder that Heckewelder became an apologist for Indians as just, generous, and civil people.

Five years later Pittsburgh's Hugh Henry Brackenridge wrote a letter more representative of white attitudes about the use of land and space. He spoke of "the animals, vulgarly called Indians," whose only claim to the soil was "occupancy." But "there is no right of primogeniture in the laws of nature and nations."

"What use do these ring, streaked, spotted and speckled cattle [the Indians] make of the soil? Do they till it?

Revelation said to man, 'Thou shalt till the ground.' This alone is human life. It is favourable to population, to science, to the information of a human mind in the worship of God.... They have the shapes of men and may be of the human species, but certainly in their present state they approach nearer the character of Devils....

In the French and Indian Wars the "Devils" had the misfortune to have chosen the French, or losing side. In the Declaration of Independence they show up not as partners in a revolution for human rights but as "merciless ... savages, whose rule of warfare is an undistinguished destruction of all ages, sexes, and conditions"—and who were being stirred and loosed on the settlers by the hated King George III.

Near the century's end more thoughtful words came from drafters of the young nation's Northwest Ordinance of 1787:

The utmost good faith shall always be observed towards the Indians; their lands and property shall never be taken from them without their consent; and in their property, rights and liberty, they shall never be invaded or disturbed, unless in just and lawful wars authorized by Congress.

Utmost good faith was never shown. In the young nation the Indians were regularly removed to the West or extinguished. The American religious map was being drawn with scant reference to the continent's first worshippers. The faith of Indian fathers lived on only on scattered reservations. The plot of religion-and-revolution developed largely without them.

With Equal Force in Favor of the Negroes

In 1700 Boston's Judge Samuel Sewall wrote a tract that suggested the seeds of a revolution in thought about religious grounds for human freedom and equality. A man clearly ahead of his time in Puritan New England, he wrote *Selling of Joseph* to attack slavery, using biblical arguments to make his case. Of the blacks on the colonies' soil, he wrote:

It is most certain that all Men, as they are the Sons of

Adam, are Coheirs; and have equal Right unto Liberty, and all other outward Comforts of Life. *GOD hath given the Earth* [with all its Commodities] unto the *Sons of* Adam, *Psal* 115.16. *And hath made of One Blood, all Nations of Men, for to dwell on all the face of the Earth....*

These Ethiopians, as black as they are; seeing they are the Sons and Daughters of the First *Adam,* the Brethren and Sisters of the Last ADAM, and the Offspring of GOD; They ought to be treated with a Respect agreeable.

"These Ethiopians" had come millennia later than had the Indians, and far from being a presence that stood between whites and open space, they were here as the result of whites' doings. As early as 1619, on the good ship *Jesus,* some accounts say, these West Africans were brought for purposes of slavery, and the slave trade continued without abatement through the century of the American Revolution. The Sewalls and the occasional Quaker men and women of courage and conviction who spoke up for slaves were rare exceptions. Even the slaveholders among the drafters of the new nation's documents about freedom and equality seldom released slaves. If any revolution was intended, the blacks were not included, in the eyes of most holders of the faith of 'our' fathers.

For twenty to thirty million Americans who are black, the question rises about *whose* father's faith is referred to. The eighteenth century saw an increase in efforts to make Christianity that faith, to supplant the African religions, most details of which were left behind when young Africans were captured and shipped into bondage. Three and a half centuries later advocates of black religion still see traces of Africanisms in the peculiar faiths developed during the years of slavery and segregation: in attitudes toward nature, peoplehood, futures, freedom, body and ritual. But a new faith was gradually if often grudgingly superimposed on the imported inheritances.

Why, it is sometimes asked, did not the black fathers and

mothers act on the logic of human freedom that was built into their faith, and take matters into their own hands? The answers are clear to any who know the logic of law and space in the eighteenth century. A revolution can occur only among people who can come to know each other to express discontent, build up courage together, and develop and respond to leaders. The slave plantation system allowed for none of these to happen, and slavery in towns also permitted little contact.

When Christian faith was taught or enjoyed among them, the slave-owner or other whites were ordinarily in close range to see that the potential for disturbance in the stories of ancient enslaved people of God would be interpreted away or avoided. Today's blacks can point to the sense of independence and identity that showed itself when black religionists were free to speak for themselves. By the 1790's, for example, the Negro freemen showed creativity as they set up churches of their own when whites denied them equality.

The northern cities were the natural sites for the expression of this freedom and ingenuity. We know of a couple of southern black congregations formed during the Revolution, but African churches experienced their surge in Philadelphia, during Constitution-writing times. Richard Allen and Absalom Jones recalled later that they were evicted from pews to galleries in a church in 1787. They stayed for prayer, but when Absalom Jones failed to stand, a white officer of the church tried to pull him up. As good dues-paying members, the blacks asserted their rights. They waited for the prayer to end and then walked out. They later passed through a kind of Quaker phase and eventually formed Allen's African Methodist Episcopal Church and Jones's Negro Episcopal congregation. Some whites were supportive of these new black efforts, but they were just as often patronizing and paternalistic. Preserved words from white sermons in these churches show how obtuse friends can be while expressing friendship.

An unfortunate by-product of the fortunate development of black churches followed, because largely-white churches now became entirely white. Fewer contacts than ever survived between the races. Winthrop Jordan in *White Over Black* says that "the new Negro churches were equal but separate, prototypes of 'separate but equal.'" Americans were learning to live with equality only if there was accompanying separation. Absence of contact made it more difficult than before for the free white majority to understand blacks and speak up with them and for them. Emancipation of slaves would have to wait seven more decades. Fulfilment of the promises of equality, freedom, and justice would be delayed and denied for still another century.

Any hint of future revolution in black status that might appear in the eighteenth century, must be spoken of as largely unintentional and almost accidental. The logic of certain Christian and 'Enlightened' ideas carried beyond the bounds of white communities and could not forever be simply contained within them. As Ebeneezer Hazard travelled through Maryland in 1777 he pointed out: "Every Argument which can be urged in Favor of our own Liberties will certainly operate with equal Force in Favor of that of the Negroes: ...nor can we with any Propriety contend for the one while we withhold the other." Nathaniel Appleton of Massachusetts, who opposed the slave market—get rid of buyers and you get rid of sellers—also shouted about this logic:

> Oh! ye sons of liberty, pause a moment, give me your ear. Is your conduct consistent? The years 1765 and 1766, will be ever memorable for the glorious stand which America has made for her Liberties; how much glory will it add to us, if at the time we are establishing Liberty for ourselves and children, we show the same regard to all mankind that come among us?

The hundreds of thousands of blacks on American shores created a dilemma from the first. While only a small minority of the colonists were church-goers, most of them felt some responsibility for Christian teaching. That teaching was clear: if a person had a soul, spiritual care was needed. Few would argue that black slaves had no souls, so whites knew that they had to provide care. The thoughtful leaders who wanted to do the providing, then had to convince slave-owners of their responsibility. Many of these feared or even observed that conversion, helpful to the slaves' soul, would be hurtful to slave owners' serenity. Christian faith and biblical stories could inspire restlessness and even revolt. What is more, whites did not like the idea that *any* kind of social distance between them and blacks might be overcome; a common Christianity represented such overcoming. In the West Indies a Reverend William Smith, the only known outspoken cleric in opposition to Negro missionary work, voiced the fear in the form of a declaration: "When a Slave is once Christened, he conceits that he ought to be upon a level with his Master, in all other respects."

Since the whites of the day were not intending revolution but only wanted for the most part to keep the status quo, they often responded with a mild counter argument. Because the Bible enjoined slaves to be obedient and would help them curb their lusts, Christianity would produce better slaves, not worse. In 1725 Dean George Berkeley stated the case from England: American planters must learn

> that it would be of Advantage to their Affairs, to have Slaves who should *obey in all Things their Masters according to the Flesh, not with Eye-Service as Men-pleasers, but in Singleness of Heart as fearing God:* That Gospel Liberty consists with temporal Servitude; and that their Slaves would only become better Slaves by being Christians.

Virginia clerics picked up and enlarged upon these themes.

The Christian faith's potential for change and freedom was also voiced in the course of the century. In the mainstream churches the major event before the Revolution itself was a series of revivals in the 1730s and 1740s, known then and now as The Great Awakening. While that Awakening was intended chiefly to lead to conversions, it carried numbers of byproducts, including the seed of antislavery opinion. Among other things, the revivals led people to a new sense of responsibility for their own self-examination and the discernment of their sins. And slavery began to be regarded more frequently not simply as economic policy but as sin.

While far from sounding like the language of modern civil rights leaders, occasional Great Awakeners' speech began to show some sense of guilt and then hope for freedom. Thus Samuel Hopkins, a protégé of Jonathan Edwards, spoke up for "universal, disinterested benevolence" in place of the self-centeredness that permitted slavery. In 1770 Hopkins, who had been converted in the 1740s, moved to Newport, Rhode Island, where he linked up with Ezra Stiles, who later became Yale's president, to work for missionary colonization of freed blacks in Africa. Even he and his kind, however, could be seen as caring more for colonization and conversion at a distance than for freedom and equality close to home. Hopkins did believe, however, that the Continental Congress's ban on the importing of slaves should lead to abolition of slavery and thus to a 'thoroughgoing reformation.'

In the eighteenth century the more revolutionary seeds and germs were often planted by the churches that did not belong to the mainstream. In the case of the black cause, the Quaker dissenters who had come from England into Pennsylvania and elsewhere, were most notable. They wanted to show that blacks were capable of expressing intelligence on the level of whites, and found an ideal exemplar of their controversial thesis in Phyllis Wheatley. She held qualifications that now as then would have made her attractive: she was young, gifted, black, and, of course, female. The Marquis de Barbé-Margois, a French official in Revolutionary America, spoke of her as "one of the strangest creatures in the country and perhaps in the whole world."

Phyllis is a negress, born in Africa, brought to Boston at the age of ten, and sold to a citizen of that city. She learned English with unusual ease, eagerly read and reread the Bible, the only book which had been put in her hands, became steeped in the poetic images of which it is full, and at the age of seventeen published a number of poems in which there is imagination, poetry, and zeal, though no correctness nor order nor interest. I read them with some surprise.

Five editions of her book, which his comment correctly appraised, appeared before 1800. The case for equality was rather slender in so far as it relied alone upon Phyllis Wheatley. More advocates speculated about environmentalism and physical causes to explain what was believed to be blacks' lesser ability and development. Appeals came to be made more frequently to Nature than to the Bible to explain black/white differences.

The Quakers were persistent, however, in grounding their own case in Christian faith. By 1768 one of them, Anthony Benezet, was regarded as the colonies' most articulate critic of slavery. More effective in the end, however, was John Woolman, one of the rare colonials whom most later observers have not hesitated to describe as being both saintly and wise. When he was asked to write a bill of sale for a slave in 1743 he experienced a sudden awakening to the issue. He then began a career of speaking up for black freedom. Woolman saw the dangers of slavery to white consciousness. In a pamphlet published in 1754 he wrote:

Being concerned with a People so situated that they have no Voice to plead their own Cause, there's Danger of using ourselves to an undisturbed Partiality, till, by long Custom, the Mind becomes reconciled with it, and the Judgment itself infected.

The Quakers came to argue that slavery was sinful because it moved the master to a sense of luxury and immorality, because the slave was pushed into sinful situations, and because spiritual bonds between both were broken. Such arguments had moved far beyond the old Puritan contentment with the subordination of slaves as being part of divine decrees.

The American Revolution was at least temporarily beneficial to many blacks. Some won their freedom by fighting in the military cause. They had not always been welcomed in the armies, but were needed, and often distinguished themselves there. Later generations of blacks have been able to point to this record to show how their forefathers had earned their right to full participation in the life of the nation. Concurrent with the Revolution there occurred also a secularizing of ideas that took both the Awakened Christians' ideas of sin and responsibility and the Quaker ideas of brotherhood a step further to permit the development of an even broader sense of equalitarianism. By the century's conclusion, however, the largely unintended revolution in ideas about equality for blacks was only beginning; it has not been fulfilled two centuries later.

The Jewish Nation and the Infidel Law

Eighteenth century Americans knew so few Jews that it seems almost artificial to include them in the story of the faith of anyone's father—except Jews' own. Many people are interested in tracing every detail of their own heritage. Some American Jews, therefore, make much of a September morning in 1654 when twenty-three shivering Sephardic (Spanish-background Jews) were brought to New Amsterdam on a French ship, the *St. Charles.* They were ancestors in faith and race of two million of today's New Yorkers and three or more million Americans elsewhere. But the original little colony did not amount to much. They had been put out of Europe and had come to find that even in Brazilian exile they were not safe. Maybe the New Amsterdam Dutch would treat them better.

Peter Stuyvesant was governor in those days; his zone of

tolerance was rather narrow. In the finest American "dammit, there goes our neighborhood" tradition, he complained that while it may be true that these new Jews might help produce prosperity in the New Netherlands, if he gave them a place, "we cannot then refuse the Lutherans and the Papists." But the Jews remained and did prosper, though by the end of the eighteenth century they made up only one twentieth of one per cent of the thirteen colonies' population—down from one tenth of one per cent at the time of the Revolution. Three thousand people are not well poised to make much of an impact on three million. The Jews, in a way, did.

Their story has been webbed with that of the rest of America quite literally from the precise beginning—at least for those who take Columbus as that beginning. Sephardic Jews had thrived under Muslim Moorish rule in Spain, but their Christian successors were less tolerant. In the time of the Inquisition it pleased Queen Isabella to convince herself that Spain would be better off without them. The deadline for the departure of Spain's last Jews was August 2, 1492. One day later Christopher Columbus—who some of the mythmakers later claimed was himself a Jew—departed for what came to be his voyage of American discovery. Those who like to record 'firsts' continue their theme: Luis de Torres, a Marrano with linguistic skills was one of the first two in Columbus' party to go ashore, while Rodrigo de Triana, one of the four other known Jews on the ships, was first to sight land.

That was long ago, in the eyes of the eighteenth century people, most of whom would not have cared about legends of firsts and who may hardly have been aware of the presence of a mere three thousand colonials not of Christian stock. Those few Jews, however, began to lead to a rewriting of the assumptions of American life. Without their presence it is quite likely that language about the United States being officially a Christian nation would have been noised further abroad and resounded louder and longer than it was. Even so, efforts have still been made to see America grounded officially in Christian faith.

While Jews were few, some dimensions of the faith of Jewish fathers and mothers was anything but unfamiliar to the biblical literates among the colonists. The New Testament, marked by a strong sense of urgency about the end of history, is a frail document in which to base political life. But the Old Testament, rich in its description of the covenanted life of the people of God, served well as a charter for colonial covenants. This was true particularly in New England, where every nuance of social life had to be rooted in these scriptures that were common to Christians and Jews alike.

Because the Hebrew scriptures were canon and code for so much colonial life, the Hebrew language was cherished. Cotton Mather, adept since age twelve in the use of the language, wrote a six-volume history of the Jews. Harvard included Hebrew in its curriculum, and well into the nineteenth century commencements at the university included a Hebrew oration. Ezra Stiles, Yale's president after 1777, held similarly high views of the language and the scriptures. New Englanders saw themselves as chosen people, led out of slavery, sometimes exiled, sent into a wilderness; some even explained the American Indians as heirs of the "Lost Ten Tribes" of ancient Israel.

A familiarity with Hebrew and Hebrews at a distance did not necessarily mean that the colonists would always welcome them next door. In nine of thirteen colonies at the time of the Revolution either Congregationalism or Episcopalianism was the established religion. Neither of these wanted much to do with Papists, Baptists and Anabaptists, Quakers, or other sects—how could they tolerate a Jewish presence? Yet, perhaps because the Jewish community was so small and so localized in a few petit-urban communities, it seemed to represent little threat. Jews often contributed to commercial prosperity; who would then look for a doctrine with which to wish or whisk them away? The larger scale anti-Semitism that afflicted sixteenth century Spain and later the rest of Europe showed up in more virulent forms in América only in the 1880s, when many Eastern European Jews began to arrive.

The Jew did represent some problems, however. At the beginning of the century, religious toleration was still a rather rare idea. The Glorious Revolution in England had permitted the first glimmers of legalized toleration there after 1689. In most American colonies it would not yet have occurred to people to develop a sense of true religious liberty for other Christians, to say nothing of Jews. Colonists had come here to win freedom for themselves. Faiths of others could be represented in other colonies—and even there they would be subject to the threat of missionary activity and attempts at conversion. The Jews and their scriptures made up part of the plot of a two-act drama in whose second act they no longer had a part of their own.

The tireless Cotton Mather, who thought of everything, thought of directing some of his ministry to conversion:

This Day [in 1696], from the Dust, where I lay prostrate, before the Lord, I lifted up my Cries...For the Conversion of the *Jewish Nation*, and for my own having the Happiness, at some Time or other, to baptise a *Jew*, that should be my Ministry, bee brought home unto the Lord.

He sent a book to an "infidel *Jew*." Its title: *Faith of the Fathers*.

The Jews in colonial America saw things differently; they were not infidel at all, but civic folk who practiced what has been called 'dignified orthodoxy' in their worship. As the eighteenth century moved on, the Sephardic forms of worship tended to survive, even though most Jews who came everywhere but to Newport, Rhode Island were Ashkenazic, a word from Genesis (10:3) that Spanish Jews used to depict German Jews and which Germans applied to Eastern

European Jews. (The Ashkenazic expression tended to be looked down upon by Sephardic elitists).

The Newport colony provides the best glimpse of Jewish life in the eighteenth century, since New York then had perhaps only thirty families and Boston may have had as few as four. Newport was hospitable to Jews. It had been founded by dissenters, most of them Baptists, as part of a colony that assured religious freedom to all. Whether that 'all' was intended to include non-Christians or not, the terms were conveniently stretched to cover the Jewish case. As a seaport, Newport offered opportunities to Jews, and they came to be considered as assets. The size of the group there crested around 1760. At about that time a synagogue was built, named Touro after Isaac de Abraham Touro, the first *hazzan* (a prayer-chanter) there. Tiny congregation Shearith Israel in New York helped financially. To this day the Touro Synagogue is a much-visited architectural jewel, a monument to simple colonial styles at their best.

The synagogues all lacked rabbis; there were only three known rabbis in the northern half of the Western hemisphere by the time of the American Revolution. Jewish intellectuals and scholars had few reasons to leave Europe for these more primitive shores. The communities were, in a way, leaderless and thus further deprived of ability to have much impact on American life. Yet the instincts of the colonial Jews served them well. They largely identified with the patriot side. Some say in retrospect that they sensed more freedom and equality in the colonial than in the imperial cause. They had no reason for ties to England.

Like most other American groups, later Jews look back to find heroes in the Revolution, people who help them further establish their claim that they are identified fully with the United States. Haym Salomon, who left Poland in 1772, fills that role. He had known Pulaski, the Polish revolutionary leader, and Kosciusko, and took up with the militant Sons of Liberty in America. The British tried to use him as an interpreter, but he worked secretly against their interests. They caught him. He escaped, to become "freedom's financier." At times he even later subsidized the salaries of James Madison and Thomas Jefferson when Treasury funds ran low. A faithful practicing Jew, he helped establish a synagogue in Philadelphia in 1783.

The Jews, who had intended only to find a place where they could live undisturbed by not making waves, thus found themselves having to choose sides in a Revolution. Their contribution to later American religious life came on grounds other than those of wartime activities. As the nation was being founded, they saw themselves excluded from full civic life by several state constitutions. They joined others in a decades-long effort to see the removal of the Christian Trinitarian clauses in the constitutions and helped enlarge the definition of religious freedom. They have joined the Quakers, the Unitarians, and other groups of whom it is often said, "They have been influential far beyond their numbers."

You and All Your Tribes

Though American Indians, Negroes, and Jews were not able to play a major part in the religious awakening or nation-building of the eighteenth century, the cast of characters for the two-part drama still remained large. This does not mean that most of the remaining population were directly involved as members of religious groups. Far from being a scene of strong church participation, both Europe and the American colonies were seeing many kinds of decline. If today around 60% of the citizens of the United States are on the rolls of churches and synagogues, perhaps only about ten per cent were at the time of the nation's birth. At the beginning of the eighteenth century the figure was already not impressive.

Low church membership and attendance figures do not tell the whole story. Most original settlers came from established European churches or quickly established religions here. This meant that the culture itself—its laws, educational agencies, sub-communities, behavior patterns, and literary symbols— often kept Christian themes on the public mind. But after everything compensatory has been said, it is clear that around 1700 few signs appeared to suggest that the next decades would see revolutions in the way people thought of the act of becoming and being religious or the act of being and becoming a free nation.

Most of the story of early eighteenth century religion in the colonies centers on three groups. As late as 1783 Yale's astute and observing President Ezra Stiles could look ahead and, without seeming to be foolish, envision an American future divided largely between Congregationalists, Presbyterians, and Episcopalians. Today none of these are sufficiently concentrated geographically anywhere to "lord it over" their environment. They remain a "thin spread" on the religious map. They exercise an influence beyond their numbers, but by no means do they hold the allegiance of statistically-impressive populations. Stiles' vision was plausible, for these churches were established in nine of the thirteen original colonies and the Episcopalians and Presbyterians were well-represented in the middle colonies, where there was no establishment.

To Stiles, the Indian, Negro, or Jewish religions would never be more than objects of curiosity; they would not have much influence on national destiny. But he could also, without damage to his subsequent reputation, overlook Roman Catholics. In the middle of the nineteenth century they became and remained the largest religious group. They were insignificantly small in his time. He could pass over Baptists and Methodists, whose size spurted immediately after he looked ahead. They became the second and third largest churches. He needed to pay no notice to the fourth largest cluster, the Lutherans, to say nothing of the various dissenting and disturbing sects that later came to thrive in the United States.

If Stiles could neglect such groups, other generations cannot. The story of the eighteenth century awakenings and, even more, the revolution, must include them, though almost no member of theirs was then making sounds or giving signs that they were ready for such a drama. Most of them were concerned chiefly with survival in a bewildering and hostile environment. Or they simply wanted to go about quietly serving their God. If later Americans were to speak of a "mainstream" or "mainline" of churches, they were outside it, unaware of their potential in the epic.

Among these the Germans, both Lutheran and Reformed, deserve notice. The Lutherans became the fifth-largest group by the end of the colonial period. The Baptists had passed them on the way to competing with "the big three." Colonial religionists were consistently and firmly Protestant. Luther, therefore, was well-regarded as an originator of Protestantism and the Lutherans were esteemed as heirs of the first large Protestant church. While some of their doctrinal positions were at variance with those of Reformed and Anglican Christianity, they were not sufficiently different to create extraordinary disturbance. The dominating three lived with equally great differences between each other.

The Germans, and especially the Lutherans, did not fit in, despite these assets. They concentrated in the middle colonies, and especially Pennsylvania. The established religious people mistrusted what was going on in that strange mix produced by Pennsylvania, New York, Delaware, and New Jersey. The idea of *not* being established, of not having a legally privileged position, was unsettling. Second, most of the Lutherans were artisans or back-country immigrants. There were among them few people of wealth, note, or learning. Most of all, they spoke a foreign language and represented an alien ethnic stock.

The ethnic character of Lutheran and Reformed Germans has been treated ambiguously in American history. By the nineteenth century, the textbooks were admiring Germans second only to English-Scotch-Irish types, because they were the mythical founders of democracy ("in the forests of Germany . . .") and because they seemed more attractive than their southern and Eastern European counterparts. By the end of the eighteenth century some observers could already be charitable. A famed French settler, J. Hector St. John Crèvecoeur, perhaps not of preferred stock himself, wrote of the Germans as being the people most at home in the primitive lands.

> How much wiser, in general, the honest Germans than almost all other Europeans; they hire themselves to some of their wealthy landsmen, and in that apprenticeship learn everything that is necessary. . . . Their astonishment at their first arrival from Germany is very great — it is to them a dream; . . . The recollection of their former poverty and slavery never quits them as long as they live.

They had to win this good reputation, and did not become secure in it. The first impressions had been less congenial. When hordes of suffering and persecuted Germans came from Germany's Palatinate to Pennsylvania, establishmentarian Benjamin Franklin in 1751 indulged in some undemocratic harrumphing:

> Why should the Palatine Boors be suffered to swarm into our Settlements, and by herding together establish their Language and Manners to the Exclusion of ours? Why should Pennsylvania, founded by the English, become a Colony of *Aliens,* who will shortly be so numerous as to Germanize us instead of our Anglifying them, and will never adopt out Language or Customs, any more than they can acquire our Complexion.

The Lutherans among them were anything but ready for awakening and revolution. The better-off Germans often shared the polite mild rationalism of their parent churches. Theirs was a "don't rattle the beer steins" kind of faith. Others were equally mild pietists. They practiced fervent personal religion but, as Lutherans, did not share the assumptions about conversion that characterized revivalism later and elsewhere. So far as revolutionary impulses were concerned, ever since the time of Luther his churches had been loyal and docile in the face of "the powers that be." If they were political at all, they tended to support the authorities that had legitimacy, and were not ready to help with any overturning.

Misfits they were, but the troubles in Germany kept forcing them to come just as the American attractions grew. They did little missionary work outside their national group and not much within it—until 1742, when the genius-founder, Henry Melchior Muhlenberg, arrived in Philadelphia. Their growth came largely from immigration. In 1700 the colonies knew only seven Lutheran churches; by 1740 there were 95 and by 1780 the number had grown to 240. The Palatinate migrations helped produce 26 New York and 19 New Jersey churches. In 1730 alone 21 new churches were started. By 1750, a year before Franklin grumbled, there were about 60,000 Lutherans in Pennsylvania.

They had not been welcome in Dutch New York. The authorities there had been reluctant to admit Jews because then they would have to recognize the Lutherans and papists who were, presumably, worse. But New York later had no principle for keeping them out. They also spilled through Maryland into Virginia. In 1731 the Archbishop of Salzburg forced the Lutherans out of his territory. Many of them came to James Oglethorpe's hospitable Georgia.

The Lutherans minded their own business. Their congregations served as centers for worship, teaching, nurture of the young, and social life, but not so much for winning the soul of the colonies or making direct contributions to the social order. To a slightly lesser extent the same was true of the German Reformed, who were as unacceptable ethnically as the Lutherans to people like Franklin. Their theology and churchmanship were more congenial to their English cousins of Reformed faith in the American majority. They did not survive in as large a churchly presence as did the Lutherans.

Through a number of mergers (Evangelical plus Reformed) they linked up in the 1950s with non-German Congregationalists to form The United Church of Christ. As Reformed, they were in colonial times more inclined to be ecumenical than were the Lutherans—though many Lutherans of Swedish, Dutch, and German background did blend and eventually meld into the Episcopal churches as they began to speak English and when they found little leadership from their own groups.

Theodore Jacobus Frelinghuysen, an illustration of the Reformed churches' ability to adapt, in 1726 was an instigator of the Great Awakening in New Jersey. The New Jersey Reformed carried on missionary activities, established the New Brunswick Seminary and Rutgers University, and were a more public presence than were their Lutheran rivals. But the Reformed were also losing place. The Dutch, who had been the established church in New Netherlands, kept yielding space to the Episcopalians and others. In 1697 Trinity Church in New York became a threat to Dutch Reformed hegemony. New York was doomed to be pluralist, and there were not enough new Dutch or practicing Reformed people to help them hold power.

***

If the Lutherans suffered legal strictures in earlier New Netherlands or were snobbed out in Franklin's era, these proscriptions were as nothing compared to what happened to the Roman Catholics in America. They were everywhere a despised tiny minority, regarded as true aliens, legally inhibited or proscribed, never welcomed, constantly mistrusted. European religious wars were just ending, and bad memories lingered on in the New World. Any signs of positive regard for modernity by the Vatican were still more than two centuries off. No record of loyal participation in political life on the part of the Catholic minority existed as there would in the nineteenth century, when prejudice still lingered on, or in the twentieth, when it died slowly.

The Protestants thought it was an act of Providence that

God had hid the northern part of the Western hemisphere from European eyes until the Reformation had occurred. Whatever had been responsible, at the very least an accident of empires' fortunes, the thirteen colonies just barely turned out to be a northwest European (Dutch, Swedish, German) and English settlement or founding and not a Roman Catholic one. A century earlier European destiny had seemed to be in the hands of Iberians from Spain and Portugal, who remained dominant in Central and South America. Or, on through the eighteenth century, the French represented a threat, though after mid-century it was clear that they would not win the interior and would have to settle for Eastern Canada. Thus Spanish and French Catholics to the south and north represented a kind of pincers to English Protestant colonists, and were regarded as ominous. They were not to be encouraged to settle their spiritual kin, English Catholics, in the English colonies.

Skirmishes and conflicts were frequent. The century opened with Georgians' attacks in 1702 on the Spanish stronghold at St. Augustine, Florida. Tension crested with "The French and Indian Wars" in the 1750s. By 1750 not a single Catholic Church survived in New England, nor were there any in Virginia, the Carolinas, or Georgia. In New England John Foxe's *Book of Martyrs* remained the most popular work in church history; it was used to instill anti-Catholic sentiment just as it inspired awe for mainly English Protestant martyrs.

New York was no more hospitable. Whereas once Catholic missionaries had distinguished themselves working among the Iroquois, in the first half of the eighteenth century there was only one Catholic parish in the colony, a spill-over across the border from Catholic Quebec. In 1700 New York had passed a law against Jesuits and "popish missionaries," designed to force all priests out by November 1 of that year. Where things mattered, near New York City, a Reverend Backhouse could write, in 1748 "There is not in New York the least face of popery." Laws against Catholics were to remain on the books there through a Constitutional revision of 1801 and even until 1806, though these restrictions were largely civil and not ecclesiastical after 1777. Only in Maryland and Pennsylvania were the few Catholics somewhat at home. In 1708 2,974 of the 33,883 Marylanders were said to be Catholic. In 1750 this number had grown to 7,692 out of 92,308, thanks in part to new migrations and the activities of occasional travelling missionary priests. The suppression of the Jesuits by the papacy itself in 1773 later deprived such colonists of an elite corps, but other religious orders took up the resulting slack. Yet even in Maryland, which had been founded by the Roman Catholic Lord Baltimore, and where Catholics first knew toleration in the colonies, matters had grown worse.

In the "penal era," a legal code was developed to shadow or parallel the anti-Catholic attitudes of Mother England. Governor John Seymour, personally a strong anti-Catholic, arrived in 1703. He inspired legislation and persecution. As of 1704 a Catholic priest was not allowed to engage in public activities there, at pain of imprisonment and eventual banishment. Only a "private family of the Romish communion" could host a religious service. Fines were levied against those who imported Irish servants. It should be said that private citizens among the Protestants worked around and softened the intent of these and other harassing measures, but Catholicism was anything but ready to play a positive public part in the century's events.

Despite the handicaps, Catholicism endured. For one thing, among the few Catholics there were some rather well-off tobacco-growing families. A certain Charles Carroll, who wanted to plead the case of some Jesuits in 1704, was the grandfather of the first Catholic in the eighteenth century to be remembered in the general history books—the Charles Carroll who signed the Declaration of Independence. Catholics were able somehow to establish a couple of institutions of learning.

There were also losses and handicaps. A psychological

blow resulted from the conversion to Protestantism of the fourth Lord Baltimore, Benedict Leonard Calvert. Catholic indentured servants, who were expected to observe about thirty days of holy obligation each year, were in constant trouble with their masters. Life could never be easy for people who lived under legislation like that of 1704's "An Act to Prevent the Growth of Popery" or who had to endure the words of Governor Seymour in the same year:

> Gentlemen, it is the unhappy temper of you and all your tribe to grow insolent under civility . . . Yet of all people, you have the least reason for considering that if the necessary laws that are made were let loose to crush you . . . you would need to dread. . . . If you intend to live here let me have no more of ["Mass-mongering"], for if I do, and [charges] are made against you, be assured I'll chastise you. . . . Pray take notice that I am an English Protestant Gentleman, and can never equivocate.

As Maryland harassed Catholics, Pennsylvania with its more genial Quaker policies, was more tolerant. By the 1700s Catholics were free to engage in public worship. In 1741 a newly arrived Philadelphia Jesuit from England could write his superior: "We have at present all liberty imaginable in the exercise of our business, and are not esteemed, but reverenced, as I may say, by the better sort of people." Such experiences were too local to indicate enough freedom that colonial Catholics could expand, revive, or share in a political revolution. And except for some "better sort of people" in Pennsylvania, non-Catholics gave almost no evidence that they and their grandchildren of the 1770s would be participating in a revolutionary change in inter-religious situations or in the extension of religious freedom among these "aliens" and "tribes."

***

Awakenings and revolution are unthinkable without the Baptists, today America's second largest religious cluster. No one contributed more to or profited more from later awakenings and revivals than did Methodists, now the third largest. They did not yet register with Ezra Stiles in 1783 and with others in the mainstream through most of the century, nor would they have been regarded as important positive forces. Methodism, of course, was not yet a presence early in the century and did not officially organize in America until 1784, so it could not become much in the eighteenth century theme.

Baptists, however, were beginning to come on the scene—though often they were regarded as alien tribes to established Christian majorities in this period. The Baptists had organized as dissenters against New England Congregationalism and had helped found Rhode Island. The number of Baptist churches (four in 1660) had grown to 33 in 1700. Since by 1740 there were 96 and in 1780 there were 457, it can be seen that Baptists prospered during the Great Awakening. The main motifs of their story belong to and can be treated both with the Awakening and the story of the Revolution. Situating them at the century's beginning, however, is an act that will further illustrate the static concepts of religion held by religious majorities in a time before awakenings and revolution.

The Baptists were numerically weak in 1700, and they were also internally divided. Some were Arminian and some were Calvinist—meaning that they had differing views of God and human beings and grace. While all did baptize adults upon profession of faith and did so by immersion, they did not agree on other rites, such as the "laying on of hands." While all were congregational in polity, some were more ready for voluntary inter-congregational 'associational' life than others. Some were influenced by English Baptists and others remained almost pure-form home-growns. Only a few were aware of continental Anabaptist roots at all. Some valued learning and literacy and others were quite primitive in their understanding of faith and culture. Most were slow to get together; not until 1707 with the Philadelphia Association was there effective organization, and that local embodiment was unique for half a century.

The Baptists, in short, were Protean and sprawling, both firm within and adaptive to many cultures. So they became the most widespread of all religious groups by 1750. A map of their churches in that year finds them nettling the Massachusetts establishment, remaining most powerful in Rhode Island, still causing schism in Connecticut congregations, toe-holding in New York, clustering around Charleston in South Carolina but spreading across North Carolina, beginning to dot Virginia, and represented in Delaware and Maryland. That left New Jersey, where over a dozen Baptist congregations were active and, most of all, Pennsylvania, which had to make room for everybody. The big push into the south came after that period, as the result of some new migrations from England but most of all because of aggressive activities by New Englanders.

With their unsettling presence in most colonies, the Baptists also had one thing else in common: they were not welcome by establishments. They were harbingers of the new day, anticipating many of the aggressive movements for change that characterized the rest of the century. For them, awakenings and revolution were not accidental events as they were for many other non-mainstream churches. They simply did not yet look powerful or promising enough to have much more than a negative impact.

Another group that people with hindsight could later say were ahead of their time as agents of change were the Quakers. They were to lose place drastically after the Revolution, but they enjoyed one century of influence. Again and again the Quakers have been seen as being out of step with other colonials, who looked backward or cherished the status quo. They had a vision of common humanity that included the Indian. They represented much of the early anti-slavery force. Their colony, Quaker William Penn's "Holy

Experiment" of 1682, was more hospitable to Jews, Lutherans, Reformed, Catholics, and Baptists—to say nothing of small sects—than was any other. For them a kind of spiritual and even political revolution was anything but fully unintended or accidental.

The Quakers, heirs of George Fox's dissenting Puritan experience of the Spirit in England, were a people of "concern" who looked for "that of God in everyman." They seemed to have believed that the Spirit's enlightenment would spread very fast through them. They could afford to welcome anyone into their colonies, because they were confident that even without aggressive proselytizing people would come to see the light. It turned out otherwise. Even some Quakers themselves or their children stopped seeing the light. Some of them, particularly in Philadelphia, saw the light of Anglican serenity and status and jumped to it. Their dissent and their pacifism—which made the act of running a colony in the presence of Indians most difficult, along with their simplicity, were all threatened by material prosperity, the temptations of power politics, and the pluralist environment they had helped create.

Samuel Fothergill, visiting from England, observed this change which prevented Quakers from being Great Awakeners. In 1756 he wrote:

> Their fathers came into the country and bought large tracts of land for a trifle; their sons found large estates come into their possession, and a profession of religion which was partly national, which descended like a patrimony from their fathers, and cost as little. They settled in ease and affluence, and whilst they made the barren wilderness a fruitful field, suffered the plantation of God to be as a field uncultivated, and a desert ... A people who had thus beat their swords into plowshares with the bent of their spirits to this world, could not instruct their offspring in the statues they had themselves forgotten.

Increasingly forgotten was the dream of William Penn:

And thou, Philadelphia, the virgin settlement of this province, named before thou wert born, what love, what care, what service and what travail have there been to bring thee forth and preserve thee from such as would abuse and defile thee.

Most of the abusing and defiling came from without for non-Pennsylvanian Quakers. But their times of overt persecution in New England belonged more to the past. In 1760 Ezra Stiles estimated that 16,000 of them lived on in New England. In the strongholds of New Jersey and Pennsylvania, perhaps 50,000 were present by century's end. They were not free to bear arms, but they could wield pens and use voices to speak up for liberties, and for this they are best remembered.

Finally, the small German peace sects were known in Pennsylvania but they made almost no dent at all on those in the mainstream. If they were known elsewhere, they were regarded as simple, backward, backwoods people who shared the Quakers' strange views about fighting wars against the Indians, French, and English. But in Pennsylvania they were visible. Mennonites and Amish, perhaps 10,000 in all, had come from Switzerland and Germany, to carry on the work of the left-wing sixteenth century reformers. They probably made up about one-tenth of the German third in Pennsylvania's population.

They played some part in the century's changing assumptions, not through their public activities or their programming for bringing about a free society, but because they forced others to reckon with the logic of documents that offered toleration to all. In the year that William Penn died, 1718, he received a letter from Mennonites in his colony:

We came to Pennsylvania to seek an asylum from the persecution to which we had been subjected in Europe. We knew the character of William Penn, and rejoiced God had made such a man.... We came to Pennsylvania to enjoy freedom of mind and body... We ask you for permission to pass our lives in innocence and tranquility. Let us pursue our avocations unmolested.

For the most part, they were both unmolested and overlooked. Similarly, the Brethren, also called Dunkers, the German Baptist Brethren, came largely between 1719 and 1736 to live out their concepts of pietism and pacifism. They were more vocal, particularly because a father and son team both named Christopher Saur had a printing press, an impulse to translate and write and publish, and the ability to propagate. Their efforts made the non-Quaker pacifist presence more familiar to other colonists. Another small group, The Schwenkfelders, traced their own roots back to a spiritualistic reformer of the sixteenth century, and were sheltered in Pennsylvania. These groups all contributed little in an active way beyond their own circles. Those circles, however, had to be reckoned with by leaders of thirteen colonies—and with important consequences.

2

The Direct Participants

Neither Soaring too High nor Drooping too Low

If the two-phased revolution in eighteenth century American religion was unintentional and, in part, accidental, the case must be made while including the Church of England or Episcopalian Church. The German Reformed and Lutheran, the Quakers, the Mennonites and Brethren and Dunkers might all have been all right in their place. But their place tended to be small or removed from scenes of power when compared with that of Episcopalianism.

The Church of England dominated the southern colonies and came to be established in all of them. In 1750 the privileged church of the northern colonies, Congregationalism, was totally unrepresented in the southern domain beyond the confines of Charleston, South Carolina. Laws of various sorts also inhibited the development—though they could not prohibit the eventual spread—of dissent. In those southern colonies the Church of England was simply a part of the way of life that played a decisive role in the great religious changes.

To this day mention Great Awakenings, revivals, evangelism, and conversion and an informed American may very well think at once of the South. "The Bible Belt" is a largely southern phenomenon; the Second Great Awakening at the beginning of the nineteenth century was most successful and pervasive there. But the Great Awakening in America was not born on Church of England soil nor nurtured under Episcopal auspices. In book after book on the southern Episcopal experience, one kind of assertion comes with predictable frequency. A random illustration is Raymond W. Albright's in *A History of the Protestant Episcopal Church:* "... the Great Awakening had come to Virginia with little approval and often open opposition by the Anglicans. Only Devereux Jarratt ... seemed to be touched by the movement." 1985741

"Only Devereux Jarratt ..." Revisionists and critics scour the southern records and find traces here and there of Anglican awakeners who might remove his name from that characteristic splendid isolation. "Only" is a word historians should use sparingly. But the fact that it comes up so regularly provides an indication of the general lack of interest in and antagonism to the Awakening in southern Episcopalianism. The northern case was hardly different, for the Church of England made its gains there precisely among the people who had no taste for the revivals that were stirring people up all around them. One of the great alterations in American religious sensibility was occurring, yet "only Devereux Jarratt" is mentioned in the general histories. His involvements were quite late. "After ordination in 1762 he took a small parish where seven or eight older persons communed and by patient teaching built a congregation of nine hundred.... Jarratt was rather shabbily treated by his colleagues but served the church well until his death in 1801." Episcopalianism went through the whole century largely untouched positively by its chief religious event. The church's participations were reluctant, rare, grudging at best—certainly never part of intention or design.

So far as the public event that absorbed religious energies is concerned, the combined acts of Revolution and nation-building, there is no question but that the Episcopalians were at the center. To begin at the end of the story, here is a summary judgment on its members' part, by historian Daniel

J. Boorstin, who tends to favor the Anglican style over the more fervent faiths of the era:

It would have been strange had not the political and social leaders of Virginia been leading Anglicans. Of the more than a hundred members of the Virginia constitutional convention of 1776, only three were not vestrymen. Two-thirds of all the signers of the Declaration of Independence were members of the Established Church; six were sons or grandsons of its clergymen. During the Revolution the movement toward resistance and independence flourished in the Virginia vestries. . . . It is hard to name a leader of the Revolution, including such men as George Washington, James Madison, Edmund Pendleton, and Patrick Henry, who were not securely within the fold of the Church. The fact that there were also outspoken Loyalists . . . who were loyal Anglicans does not alter the case. For in Virginia a quiet devotion to the English Church—both as a bulwark of things ancient and English and as a local expression of the passion for independence—nourished that very reverence for the British constitution and for the traditional rights of Englishmen which inspired the Revolution. There is no paradox then in the facts that the leaders of Virginia were almost to a man good Anglicans and that these same Virginians led the Revolution.

Nothing in the design or program of the Episcopal Church in any colony would appear to predispose its members toward Revolution. The eighteenth century image of the Church, at least in the South, was one of general somnolence and, in some cases, near death. In the North, where the Episcopal exiles and converts lived outpost existences, their inclinations were often toward Toryism and Loyalism. The story of this quiet church deserves a prime place in an account of the accidental revolutions—not least of all because Episcopalianism is securely "in the American mainstream."

Revivalists and historians alike share the temptation to exaggerate the highs and lows, the ebbs and flows, the waxings and wanings, the darknesses and dawns of religious fortunes. So it may be easy to overdo the quietude in and failures of eighteenth century Episcopalianism. This has certainly been the case with England's story. In order to prepare awakened Christians or readers for the high drama of John Wesley's Methodist revival in England, people often have depicted the life of the church before his fires raged as nothing but embered. Historian Norman Sykes almost singlehandedly corrected this picture by pointing to survivals of piety and Christian vitality. But even after his book-length correcting footnotes are entered into the record, the true democrat or the pure Wesleyan would still yawn. So with the southern colonial record. Make room for the revisers and the exception-finders; despite their efforts, it would be hard to make too little of Episcopal energies.

A moderating statement concerning American Episcopalianism was voiced by the Rev. Hugh Jones, who was acquainted with Virginia. Boorstin cites him as a man after his own heart. Thus Jones in 1724:

> If New England be called a Receptacle of Dissenters, and an Amsterdam of Religion, Pennsylvania the Nursery of Quakers, Maryland the Retirement of Roman Catholics, North Carolina the Refuge of Run-aways, and South Carolina the Delight of Buccaneers and Pyrates, Virginia may be justly esteemed the happy Retreat of true Britons and true Churchmen for the most Part; neither soaring too high nor drooping too low, consequently should merit the greater Esteem and Encouragement.

The "high" and "low" to which he referred could imply high and low churchmanship—referring to relative scales of devotion to formal, official, structured church life. It could also mean degrees of fervency. No matter; it was true in either case.

In the eyes of most non-Episcopalians and to many who

deserted Episcopalianism for dissent and fervency, Jones was wrong: everything did "droop too low." There were many reasons for this drooping. As already implied, the mother Church of England in England was itself not "soaring too high." The excitements of the sixteenth century Reformation had been left far behind. The dissension caused by the Puritan revolution induced distaste for too much rigor and fervor in many sectors of England. Through the eighteenth century, the British church on which Americans would have to depend, was characterized by words like "amplitude"— everything could come into its embrace; "latitudinarianism"—a relaxed and tolerant breadth; or "Arminianism"—a theological substance and style that gave no credence to narrow definition, doctrinal strictness, or moral precisionism. Eighteenth century English Episcopalianism was a gentleperson's faith, designed for mild moral benevolence and right thinking. It was not a faith to set people afire with zeal.

If the eighteenth century Atlantic parallels were of little help, the seventeenth century legacy was even more burdensome. The southern settlers, despite impressive exceptions, had written little of a missionary sense into their charters, and had exemplified less of it in their lives. For them the concepts of having an "errand into the wilderness" or being a "citty set upon a hill," while not wholly absent, were anything but typical or central. They were explorers, venturers, traders, and eventually planters. They brought along their chaplains and a few missionaries—most of whom soon abandoned much sense of tracking down Indian converts. Not many of these were eager to go to seek lost English souls in the backwoods and backwater areas.

They brought less vision of a Kingdom or an empire of faith than did the Puritans to the north. Theirs was not a zealous and dedicated ministry to match that in Massachusetts and Connecticut. Few learned treatises issued from Virginia or Carolina parsonages, few remembered sermons from southern pulpits. Worse, the Church of England burdened its distant representatives with an unworkable polity.

Whereas Congregationalists could simply set up shop wherever a few gathered in a congregation—and could do so with full theological sanction and good conscience—and whereas people with Presbyterian or synodical policies could connect with each other on their own, the Episcopal hierarchical style forced even the most low-drooping churchmen to acknowledge the rights and tutelage of a bishop. But no bishop preceded or followed the American Episcopalians in the whole colonial period. They were nominally led by the Bishop of London. He was thousands of miles and many months of round-trip messages away. Any modern bureaucrat who can depend on instantaneous communication by telephone, wire, radio, and computerized connections, can imagine what this meant for contacts. Even today subordinates can engage in acts of incomprehension. "What did you mean?..." "Please clarify..." "Would you reconsider?..." And superiors know how they can engage in creative foot-dragging or obfuscation when their employees are only a few feet away. They can picture how inefficient contact between continents was then.

This situation was aggravated by the fact that the Bishop of London had more important and attractive things on his mind than the supervision of his wayward western flank. In effect, then, the southern colonial Episcopalians drifted into practical congregationalism. They lacked a religious basis for the drift, and might well have had a bad conscience about what they were doing. They had few of the assets and most of the liabilities of congregational patterns.

The vacuum left by the distant bishop was filled only slightly by the activities of the Governor of each colony, who was supposed to assume supervisory roles. The church had low priority on the overloaded agenda of each of these. Their supervision was often of a negative character, it appeared only in crisis, and seemed devoid of planning. The result was the almost accidental development of a vestry system that was to play a part in the unintended revolutions of the latter part of the century. If there was to be any church, someone had to "run the show" and lay elites in each parish tended to do so. Lacking nudges from above, they tended to become self-electing and self-perpetuating and thus apparently irreformable boards.

The vestrymen rapidly learned that they could easily dominate the clergy. Technically, they were supposed to "present" a priest to the governor for approval if he were to receive tenure in a parish. But once a man had tenure, he was hard to unseat and thus hard to control. The intricate politics between pulpit and pew received a great incentive. The vestrymen need do nothing more than delay, sometimes for a score of years, their "presenting," thus reducing the cleric to the status of a "hired man"—the term comes from the complainers of that era against that system.

Worse, the priest had to depend upon such leaders for financial support. He lived off "glebe" lands that the parish owned. In Virginia, for example, this meant that he was paid in tobacco. In lush areas he lived fairly well. Where tobacco was bad, he was ill-paid, and only less-qualified ministers were willing to serve in these areas of greatest need. The quality of the clergy had not been high in the first place. Until the eighteenth century mission movements began, there seemed to be no motivating system for attracting good men to bad places. And southern colonies were bad places. Many clerics who had failed or been flawed in their English parishes took American charges as last refuges and last resorts. They were rarely the kind of people who would produce awakenings and revolutions.

Nor had God or geography been good to Virginia, when the river pattern was geologically gouged, or to North Carolina, with its mountain ridges. In New England it was not hard to form towns in the flatlands and rolling hills, and to have people converge and huddle together where ministry was easy. But Virginia parishes often sprawled for many miles on both sides of hardly passable rivers. Church-going meant more than a full day's round-tripping. Few people were devoted enough to surmount the ecological obstacles. "Chapels of ease" were started on plantations. There itinerants could minister to family or clan, but congregations were formed only with difficulty. The crucial rites of passage in which religion marks the central events of life: birth, coming to adulthood, marriage, and death—were delayed or obstructed. It must be remembered that just as clerics had to pay out the equivalent of many thousands of dollars in today's money to go to the Bishop of London to be ordained, so lay people had to make a similar voyage to be confirmed by him. The obstacle course was too strenuous, and baptism often became the last rite eventually performed by the church.

Despite these handicaps the church survived and even sometimes thrived in the southern colonies, and during the eighteenth century made impressive intrusions in the north. The 41 colonial Episcopal churches of 1660 had grown to 111 in 1700; by 1740 there were 246 and in the time of the Revolution, 406. This did mean that Episcopalianism was beginning its drop from first place early in the seventeenth century to fourth place after the Revolution, a slide not interrupted by 1840 when it had dropped to seventh place. Yet it never "drooped so low" as to move out of the mainstream.

Two good things happened to the southern churches and, through them, to American Episcopalianism, right at the turn to the eighteenth century. Their names were James Blair and Thomas Bray. They were known as "commissaries," a rather secular-sounding title for their task, which was to represent the Bishop of London and take up some of the slack in the inter-continental ties. That title also had little theological legitimacy, as "Bishop" would have. But in these two instances the right person had come along to make a good post out of a bad job.

Blair was responsible for the growth in numbers of better qualified ministers and, in 1693, for the founding of the College of William and Mary, which became the beginning of an intellectual center for Episcopalianism. In 1700 Thomas Bray, who had a good clerical record in England, was settled in Maryland, though he eventually learned that he could do more for the church from England than in America. His legacy includes two impressive organizations. In 1698 he founded the Society for Promoting Christian Knowledge, which still exists. His interest was in promoting libraries and literacy in Maryland and other colonies.

Of more immediate importance was his success at getting the king to charter the Society for the Propagation of the Gospel in Foreign Parts in 1701. The SPG not only helped Episcopalianism survive in the South, but also to propagate itself in the North. Bray took pains to include Negroes and Indians in that charter, but New England's Congregationalists, not always without reason, accused the SPG of poaching, of trying to gain converts from the already churched. Between 1702 and 1783 the SPG was responsible for placing over 300 ordained missionaries in the thirteen colonies. But Bray's eventual successors as commissaries were less successful than he, and the SPCK and SPG were his monuments more than a truly healthy church in Maryland, for which he had been sent.

By 1750 the Church of England had spread quietly but remarkably through the colonies. Virginia was still the nominal stronghold, but with the weak clergy and the relatively strong vestries, it has to be described more as a place of quiet "Way of Life" religion than any kind of disturber of the peace or sphere in which new people would find meaning or a sense of belonging. South Carolina in 1700 had only one priest for the whole state beyond Charleston, and only Charleston was a lively center through much of the century. North Carolina, with its mountain ridges, geographical isolation, and dispersed and often unruly families, was a disaster area for the Episcopalians.

Georgia's church should not have suffered for lack of talent. Almost the first Anglican cleric was John Wesley, one of the few geniuses of post-Reformation Protestantism. When he arrived in 1736 he was still a high church Episcopalian; his Methodism-to-be did not show up in his rigid and unresponsive ministry. His service was ineffective, his personal relations bordered on the scandalous. He was one of the great awakeners of modern Christianity, but his less than two years in America gave no sign of that. Wesley's homecoming ship in England passed by that of a second missionary of the SPG, George Whitefield, almost his peer as a reviver of the faith. Deacon Whitefield began services in 1738 at Savannah, whence he began to become a kind of commuter between continents and Protestant faiths, a man who figured large in the story of the later Great Awakening. Despite these talents, Whitefield remained in what the second priest, Samuel Quincy, had called, when he turned around to leave it in 1735, a "mere scene of distress."

In the South the Episcopal Church, though Established by law, was least Episcopal and most Congregational. As it "trickled up" northward onto Presbyterian and then Congregational soil, it took on an ever less presbyterian (elder-run) and congregational character. In a hostile environment it developed more churchly integrity, though its members were less well-situated to play a positive part in the American Revolution. Like their southern counterparts, the new converts tended to "sit out" the Awakening and ride out or run away from the Revolution.

For the middle colonies, Episcopalians had a fortunate break just before the century began when a Quaker dissident, George Keith, converted and helped his new church make its way in Quakerdom of Pennsylvania and New Jersey. In 1703 Keith and an associate began working the New York-New Jersey-Pennsylvania circuit, where many other dissidents "came over with good zeal, and according to good knowledge, to the Church." The impressive Christ Church in Philadelphia, founded at the turn of the century, became prosperous and served as a focus for Pennsylvania Episcopalianism. As Quakers turned to the church, so did the Swedish Lutherans, who were not well served by their hierarchy in Sweden, and who found the latitudinarian style of Episcopalianism compatible. In 1702 New Jersey became a colony under the Crown and a scene of missionary activity, thanks to the ever-alert SPG.

The eighteenth century is the time in which the weak New York Anglican Church began to become strong. Trinity Church was founded in 1697, but growth beyond it was slow until mid-century when King's College, later known as Columbia, was formed in 1754. In these colonies just as the Episcopalians first grew by drawing converts from the relaxed edges of other churches, they were to lose many to the revivalists of the Great Awakening, who had more excitements to offer.

New England was the scene of higher drama. Rhode Island, hospitable to dissent, represented little official challenge to Episcopalians. The church is remembered chiefly for the seven years that Dean George Berkeley spent there after 1729. A major philosophical thinker, he was an apologist for Christianity in England and for America to English Christianity. Despairing of British church life, he looked with only faint hope to the colonies, but he did "give them a try." Despite his first plans, he stayed in "Whitehall" near Newport for those seven years, continuing to write, and now and then setting out to convert. But lacking promised English support, he returned to Britain, there to advance the colonial religious and educational causes.

The northern drama centered in Connecticut. The SPG, giving little attention to Indians, did spread the Anglican word among people of power and reached its center in 1722 at Yale College. The Berkeley library was to go there, but before that subversive act, something of more importance had occurred. Timothy Cutler, a promising young cleric and Yale's first president after it was situated to stay in New Haven, was converted. On September 12, 1722, at Commencement, Cutler greeted the post-sermon congregation with the tell-tale Anglican sign, "And let all the people say Amen!" The church that the northern colonists had fled in order to complete the Reformation and purify America was now in their bastion. Cutler lasted only a month, but he took with him Samuel Johnson, a gifted tutor. "Apostasy" was on the tongues of many. Yale graduates began to seek Anglican orders, and "Old North" Christ Church in Boston was soon to have Cutler's ministry to strengthen the growing Episcopal parish. He was to lead the requests for a bishop, especially when the Great Awakening beguiled many Anglicans.

Massachusetts was the scene of much sniping between the more liberal Congregationalists and their SPG-nurtured competitors; that conflict was to have consequences in a time when colonists were preparing their minds for the Revolution. The Episcopalians never came to majority status in the middle or northern colonies, and were to be set back by the Loyalism of many in the war just as they were to be pushed aside by the fervor of many Awakened ones before it. But they were becoming an intercolonial church, known and recognized in many locales outside the south.

It was the southern Episcopalians, however, who out of their weak churches came forth with strong persons and words in defenses of the liberties that were to be, in part, their gift to many who were never attracted to their ministries, in a Revolution few of them intended.

Slow to Grasp the Meaning of the American Situation

The second last set in the cast of characters for eighteenth century American religious change is the diverse group of people who make up Presbyterianism. Presbyterianism was truly an eighteenth century arrival and development in the colonies. In 1700 only a couple dozen congregations could be associated with the term Presbyterian in the broadest sense. Most of them did not know each other. They came from different stocks and were widely dispersed.

By 1740, during the Great Awakening, their churches came to number 160 and at the end of the Revolution their 495 congregations left them only behind the front-running Congregationalists—with whom most of them would team up in a Plan of Union in 1801. From early insignificance they had joined "the big three" within seven or eight decades. They have remained securely in the mainline of American religion—even though they, like Episcopalians and Congregationalists—dominate no single area statistically.

Beginning with several straggling Long Island groups in 1650, they also were truly an intercolonial network in 1750. They were still unrepresented in North Carolina, one of their future strongholds. Rhode Island, hospitable to everyone, had not been touched. Connecticut and Georgia had only one such church in 1750; yet there were generous clusters in Maine, New Hampshire, and Massachusetts in the North as well as in Maryland, Virginia, and South Carolina in the South. The Presbyterian stronghold was developing in the Middle Colonies. Philadelphia was often a port of entry for the transplants and the hub of converting activity for earlier arrivals who had not yet been Presbyterianized. Neither northern nor southern established churches were successful at winning the middle colonies. The Quakers were receding and Continental groups came in insufficient numbers or were handicapped by language, custom, ethos, or theology, from making advances. Presbyterianism's moment had come.

If one asks how poised it was to participate in revivals of religion or revolutions in politics, the answer is clear: it showed few signs of readiness. Leonard J. Trinterud, historian of *The Forming of an American Tradition* summarized the Presbyterian character and status just before everything broke lose; his review merits lengthy quotation:

> The conditions under which the Presbyterians labored were quite adverse. They had few strong congregations.... Out on the frontier the members of each struggling congregation were scattered over a wide area....

The people were poor, and unable to support a pastor in any adequate manner. Preachers were hard to secure.... More than one minister or candidate who came from Ireland was found to be a renegade who had forged his credentials.

The settlers to whom these Presbyterian churches ministered had come to these new frontier settlements with little vital and practical godliness. The religious life of Scotland at this time was falling more and more under control of the so-called Moderate Party. The Presbyterianism of Ulster, while intensely and polemically orthodox, was especially devoid of deep or fervent piety during this period. New England Puritanism also had lost its early zeal and spirit. On the frontier, poverty, hardship, suffering, disease, bereavements, Indian wars, sudden death all bred callousness, resentment, and cynicism. Coarseness and indecency were only too prevalent. Extreme individualism stifled brotherly kindness and mercy.... The lack of educational institutions and common social activities hindered progress within the various groups, and delayed their fusion. The fact that many of these immigrants had fled persecution at home, had come to the colonies as indentured servants, or had been deported from the homelands, only increased these antisocial attitudes.

When all the old traditions, mores, conventions, and customs of the homeland which made for a formal adherence to religion and morality were sloughed off at the frontier, indifference to the Church and even to common morals, became everywhere evident.... The social effects of irreligion, natural religion and dead polemical orthodoxies of many varieties were more apparent on the frontier, where no traditional restraints made for at least superficial morality, than they were in the old, stable communities of Europe and Great Britain.... On the whole preaching was of an order not calculated to

arouse or quicken the Church. Even of the better ministers, the great number were very slow to grasp the
meaning of the American situation. They continued to
live, think, and act as though they were still a part of
their homelands.... The frontier conditions were soon
to break down all these old orders, leaving some men to
continue living in an unreal world of yesterday while
impelling others to attempt the creation of new forms
and new orders adequate for preaching the Gospel in the
frontier situation.

These paragraphs refer to the main locales of Presbyterianism in the 1720's, just before the Great Awakening, in which
they were to take such a part in creating "new forms and new
orders."

The Presbyterians arrived to be neither awakeners nor
democrats. Their deepest theological roots lay with John
Calvin, the French-Swiss reformer whose impressive system
hardly programmed its devotees to preach for conversions or
to engender emotional responses. His concept of Geneva as a
uniform theocracy was far removed from anything that
would be possible for participants in American democracy.
The seeds for their revolutions were traceable back to Calvin,
or to some readings of Calvinism, but these were not dis-
cernible to any American friends or foes as late as the 1720s.

More immediate roots were in Scotland, where John Knox
had transplanted them as part of his completion of the Scottish Reformation. (Some Reformed Christians from Switzerland, more from the Huguenot Protestant group in France,
and occasional Netherlandish people adopted Presbyterian
order, but the British Isles were the main sending centers.)
Nothing in Knox set them up for the American changes
either. He might more readily have been the agent of their
polemics, their orthodoxy, their sense of order, their notable
sternness.

The Presbyterians had waxed and waned in sixteenth century England and lived on chiefly in Scotland. The English in

the seventeenth century tried to people Ulster, Northern Ireland, with "their kind," and found Scottish Presbyterians ready to go. These uprooted people produced a strange mixture of doughty faithful church goers and rough-and-tough displaced persons. Things went bad for the Scotch-Irish in the early eighteenth century—hence the American migrations after 1714. Blame famine, high rents, bad crops, repressive policies, persecutions, whatever; Presbyterians, the best and the worst of them, had no choice but to come to the States. Like many later arrivals, they found that the choicest land and towns in New England and the South had been preempted, and they poured through Philadelphia beyond New Jersey and Delaware into the wilds of Western Pennsylvania and then into the mid-South and the opening West. Thousands came each year; few brought ministers with them or could easily find leadership.

They were, however, Protestants of British provenance. Benjamin Franklin, who snobbed out the Germans, did not take out ethnic prejudices on them. He was to spend a great deal of time taking sides with some Presbyterians against the others, mingling outrage and sympathy, being polemical against the polemical and speaking fondly of the gentler, more literate, more sympathetic among them. The Scotch-Irish created two very distinct and different impressions, depending upon their background, status, and influences. Either they were very devout, strict and ordered or they were godless, drunken, and unruly. There seemed to be few middle of the road observers or middling perceptions.

As if their internal varieties were not enough, add an earlier, smaller lineage to the Presbyterian mix. Those two dozen seventeenth century plantings were mostly not Scottish or Scotch-Irish. They were chiefly New York (Long Island) or New England Puritans who had not been touched by much of Knox and the favored Westminster Confession, which was formative for that faith in the British Isles. Indeed, they were not much given to subscribing to creeds and confessions at all. Their theology was largely that of New England's developing Congregationalism. There was one difference, however; they did not share Congregationalists' passionate independency. They did not think each local church was sufficient unto itself. They favored "connectionalism," interaction between congregations, a kind of hierarchy of judicatories. In short, in church order they had Presbyterian sympathies.

Theological issues having to do with election and predestination; peculiar Calvinist or Knoxian views of the Lord's Supper; the finer points of Westminster—these did not attract them. They repulsed many. But they did respond to the idea of an order that saw local congregations and their "sessions" responsible to presbyteries which, in turn, made up synods that met in General Assembly. Here was a system that was designed to blend the power of laity and clergy, of the local and the translocal. As it turned out, the mixture was very well adapted to the contingencies of frontier and republican religion, though the people who chose it did not or could not have yet known that.

Presbyterians needed a catalyst or charismatic figure to bring them together. Both turned up in the figure of an Irish immigrant named Francis Makemie, who is almost always regarded as the founder in America. He arrived in 1683, to work as a wanderer in the south and in Barbados; but he also made contact with the New Englanders, notably the Mathers and other elites, on whom he made valid and valuable impressions. After appropriate scraps with Quakers, ententes with the Episcopalians, and a late tour of duty in Barbados, Makemie arrived in Virginia just before the new century began and made a trip to England in 1704. Having stirred up some support for colonial religion, he returned to Maryland and before long helped organize the first presbytery at Philadelphia. He died in 1708, having participated in only two annual meetings, in 1706 and 1707.

In the year of his death, in New England lay and clerical

delegates met at Saybrook, Connecticut, to agree on a legal document, The Saybrook Platform—which pulled the Yale and Connecticut orbits into sympathy with Middle Colony Presbyterianism both theologically and in church order. The charter was convenient for agents of the Great Awakening, but by itself it did little to revive religion.

Presbyterians being Presbyterians, conflict was inevitable. Readers of Scottish church history become used to reading of jurors and non-jurors, Burghers and anti-Burghers, Auld Lichts and New Lichts, Frees and Wee Frees, Disrupters and anti-Disrupters. Their American counterparts were no different. In the middle colonies' presbyteries, one element became ever more concerned to insist on details of order and jots and tittles of Westminster. New Englanders, even after Saybrook, were by no means ready to yield what they regarded as their Christian liberties. Nor did what turned out to be the majority in the middle colonies. They found leadership in the second great Presbyterian pioneer, Jonathan Dickinson. He favored the party that, while thoroughly conservative theologically, wanted to stress Christian experience. This party would rather examine each ministerial candidate for the character of his experimental knowledge of Christ, and then trust him. Less attractive was a kind of legalistic imposing of Westminster.

The controversy was agonizing and distracting; it issued in the Adopting Act of a synod in 1729 and, as might have been expected, settled little. The two parties went home to sulk or to agree to disagree under the cover of the superficially reconciling Act. The New England party plus the followers of the Dickinsons formed the group out of which positive Presbyterian response to the Great Awakening was to come.

Later in the century one-sixth of the white colonists would be Scotch-Irish, and many of them would be Presbyterians— joined by Presbyterians of other ethnic stock. Contentious, busy, articulate, rough-cut, they were prepared for the events that made them so quintessentially American in the century's struggles. It was a position few had sought and fewer would have understood.

A Terrible Shake unto the Churches of New England

Events do not always occur at the same pace with the same intensity in every place. The historian of early nineteenth century American religion keeps an eye on the frontier, on the expanding West. If he or she is to account for change later in the same century, the cities will receive the focus, as churches adapted to life there and the later immigrants filled them. So far as colonial America is concerned, sooner or later the needle on the historian's compass turns to New England and especially to its Congregational churches. The dramas of the Great Awakening and the religious involvement in the Revolution, however much they were shared in thirteen colonies, somehow either centered there or can there be best observed.

Today it is hard to picture why this could have been the case. The visitor to New England sees a Congregational church or its offspring, a Unitarian one, in every village and town. These monuments of the colonial era remain, and historically-minded contemporaries are glad to point them out. But New England today is not Congregational. If it is anything, it is Roman Catholic, but no single religion dominates the laws, customs, practices, or headlines as colonial Congregationalism did.

The foreign visitor would be hard pressed to discover why a fuss should be made over Congregationalism at all. Where is it? It survives in the names of some individual congregations in the United Church of Christ, or in some churches that did not go into the merger, one of at least three that were necessary to produce that denomination. But the map of American religion shows almost no counties where either the Congregational or the United Church of Christ outnumber other churches in the measuring of people's loyalties.

All through the seventeenth and eighteenth centuries Congregationalism had more congregations than anyone else. By the end of the period its closest cousin, Presbyterianism, had moved to second place, adding to their overall dominance. No one else was welcome in New England outside Rhode Island. In 1700 no church that was not Congregational existed in all Connecticut, and Massachusetts' purity was violated by only the first Anglican, one Quaker, and two Baptist churches. A year later the Society for the Propagation of the Gospel began its missionary intrusion, but statistically the picture was not drastically altered.

The 146 local churches of 1700 became 423 in number by Great Awakening times and 749 by the Revolution. This growth was concentrated in New England. In 1750 three Long Island and one other New York churches, two in New Jersey, and four in South Carolina were Congregational outposts. But through the colonial era it is almost safe to make a religious equation: New England = Congregationalism.

Numbers alone would not determine the drama. Creative minorities can change history. Thus Quakers have been few but influential beyond their numbers in American history. Other factors were pressing. These churches had civil power. They had come with and been set up by the lay elites of the Puritan colonies at Plymouth and Massachusetts Bay and later in Connecticut. A corps of well-educated, potent, articulate ministers joined them, to help set terms for the common life. What today are called "church" and "state" were not separated, nor did anyone dream of making too clear a distinction between their spheres. Those who exercised the franchise for power had to be church members. Membership was not nominal; it had to be certified by an explicit conversion experience.

No detail of life was beyond the skein of theological interpretations of the Puritans—neither laws nor marital customs, the education of children, the price of nails, the starting and placing and ordering of towns, the electing and inaugurating of civic officials. Nor were there circumstances of either

failure or success for which there were not available interpretations. Here was a theocracy in which God ruled. His word
was in a book, the Bible, which could be agreed upon by all
right-thinking free people. Elders and ministers could serve as
interpreters. Sermons expounded the truths by which the
community should live.

The picture could be overdrawn. New England had plenty
of ne'er-do-wells, lackadaisical Christians, foot-dragging
Puritans, waywards and drifting folk. Each year as more is
learned about the lives of common men and women, the
picture becomes more accurate. Not everyone jumped out of
bed on a Sabbath to hurry to church and enjoy long sermons.
Not all of them took the preacher's word without having
fingers crossed or without talking back. But if anyone departed from a norm, he or she at least knew what the norm of
the elite would be. If anyone wanted to improvise or, perish
the thought, innovate, it was not hard to know what was to
be changed. Whoever sought argument could easily find
someone armed with the official theses to defend.

So clear had been the Puritan intentions, so often had they
been articulated, so subtly had they been revised, and so
available are the documents portraying all this, that New
England has bred its enemies simply because it is felt that
other colonies deserve equal time. Committees of historians
plan conferences in which they set out to minimize colonial
New England, only to find soon that their magnetic needles
also soon turn toward Boston or New Haven. Why? Because
the Congregationalists were, well, *interesting*, that's why. The
Hawthornes and Melvilles and other great writers knew that,
too. They turned the ethos of New England into the American myth in a way that Pennsylvania Dutch folklorists or
historians of Virginia Anglicanism never could do.

Weighted and freighted as the Congregational story is,
then, one is not disappointed to find that much of the action
of the Great Awakening and the Revolution occurs in New
England. If the Awakening helped produce a new religious

ethos and develop characteristic American ways of being religious, the now-outnumbered Congregationalists who then outnumbered others have to be watched. As Revolution came, the run-of-the-mill Congregationalists, along with their uneasy "left" wing and the Baptist offspring on one hand and the liberalizing Arminian wing, soon to be Unitarian, on the other, were all involved.

The idea that the Awakening and the Revolution were largely unintended and accidental is tested only slightly in New England. Revisionist-minded historians tend to be cautious in talking about watersheds and decisive turns in history. If everyone says there was a Great Awakening, well, then, be careful. It may not have been Great just because people then and since have called it that. Maybe it did not awaken as many as it was claimed to have done, and maybe more people were awake at its outbreak than usually have been observed and counted.

Be suspicious, we are well reminded, when revivalists tell how bad everything was just before their generation whipped into action for the Lord. Rightly so. Their achievements look greater against the background of universal malaise and spiritual deadness. Many of the portrayals we have do come from the people of that time. Thus the younger Thomas Prince in his *Christian History* (1744-45) helped stamp in the minds of later generations the concept of seven preceding decades of spiritual decline. It is good to remember that faithful pastors served surviving flocks in over 400 congregations that had existed pretty much without the revivals. Nor was Puritanism entirely alien in spirit to the revival concept. *The Heart Prepared*, to cite Norman Pettit's book title, shows the Puritan sensitivity to effects, to the need for careful cultivation of the soul.

If one illustration is needed to show the latency of revivals ready to break out, none better can be found than in the career of Solomon Stoddard. His main contribution was based on the Half-Way Covenant, whose story belongs to the seventeenth century, since it was devised as early as 1662. Here it need only be recalled in a few lines as a necessary background to the Awakening. There were not enough "visible saints" in New England: piety did not pass automatically through the genes. When a new generation of those who were less religious or who had had no clear experience produced children, should these be baptized? Originally, they could not have been. But in 1662 the new arrangement regarded baptized but not professed Christians as being somehow part of the covenanted community. The parents themselves had to "own the covenant" and live uprightly, but they could not take the Lord's Supper or determine church life for others.

This compromise could not be truly satisfactory; it was designed to hold loyalties and not to vivify the church. But it was successful and its production of two classes of church members was an agreeable policy. As years passed, however, strains showed. How could the children of the Halfway Covenant come the whole way? They could not "fake it." They were not to partake unworthily of the Lord's Supper. Paul had said that those who do, eat and drink damnation unto themselves.

Enter Solomon Stoddard of Northampton, the "Pope" of the western churches, the dominant figure in the Connecticut Valley. No one can search another's heart, he reasoned. Only God knows who the true saints are. The line between a true and vivid experience and others is relative; how does one know that the more authentic believers do not have higher standards than some who profess an experience? Deal in good faith with appearances. If someone accepts a covenant or creed, forget about the line between Halfway and whole way Christians. Baptize all the community children. Absorb all the citizens at the Lord's table. The town meeting took on new importance—and he controlled that. What did this mean for the Lord's Supper? Stoddard was not casual about it; he simply stressed that it was a converting ordinance. Come, he invited, that you might have an experience.

He had begun single-entry bookkeeping on his own in the 1670's. Increase Mather sniffed: "I wish there be not teachers found in our Israel that have espoused loose large principles here, designing to bring all persons to the Lords Supper...altho' they never had Experience of a work of Regeneration in their souls." But Stoddard's success succeeded, and by 1700 he took on all comers in the effete east. More, he began to criticize the old order and its orthodoxy. Manifestly, it had failed. Who could deny it? Many of our best documents of New England's religious decline come from his charges and from the eloquent silence of the defenders. He did exclude scandalous sinners; he had some standards. But still the Lord's Table was crowded at Northampton. So far as grace was concerned, he also anticipated some of the Great Awakening themes, though his own grandson, Jonathan Edwards, pulled things back into line after Stoddard's slackening. Grace was not certifiable; you knew it only in the heart and the hunches.

These views were not too different from those of Presbyterians, who were beginning to take up some of the more tired Congregationalists' slack. Stoddard had the backing of his own people. And he boldly moved out beyond pure congregationalism and tried to establish "consociation," a new and half-Presbyterian polity. He propagated his ideas by marrying off his daughters to the area's ministers, and by flaunting his successes. He also made a great leap forward into clericalism by announcing that the minister "is made the judge by God...and it is not the work of the brethren or ruling elders, any ways to intermeddle in that affair or limit him."

Eventually he had to go beyond homefront popularity and propagation through daughters' marriages. His movement had to grow, so he took his message out to the people in evangelistic style. He preached telling sermons, fresh from his mind and into their hearts, without benefit of manuscript or notes. Counselling was time-consuming; the sermon was more efficient and authoritative. His early revivals date back to the seventeenth century, but they continued, according to his reckoning, in the time of true declension, around 1712 and 1718. "In each of them... the greatest part of the young people in the town, appeared chiefly concerned for their salvation."

Stoddard remained a Calvinist, one might almost say an old Calvinist. His God was inscrutable and arbitrary, saving whom he would. But people watched Stoddard's louder-than-word actions, in which he developed a climate predisposing people toward conversion and creating the impression that it was all up to them. Terrify people with the threat of hell, make access to heaven easy at the open Lord's table, and discipline the converts: this was his formula. His competitors had not yet learned his revivalistic key, but they learned fast in the Great Awakening. In his own time, as his great-great grandson, Yale President Timothy Dwight was later to say, he "possessed, probably, more influence than any other Clergyman in the province."

Stoddardism or Stoddardeanism was divisive, a scandal to the Boston establishment. And Stoddard the maverick poured it on. Ministers must

> get the Experience of this Work in their own Hearts. If they have not Experience, they will be but blind Guides, they will be in Great Danger to entertain false Notions concerning a Work of Conversion... Whatever Books men have read, there is a great need of experimental knowledge in a Minister.... It is a great calamity to wounded Consciences to be under the Direction of an unexperienced Minister.

He meant unexperienced, not inexperienced. The clerical battle of the Great Awakening was anticipated.

Just as there had been anticipations of revival, so the first glimmers of the churchly unrest that issued in political involvements also appeared in the career of another maverick in this period. Once again, he cannot be described as characteristic or typical and did not even acquire the kind of power Stoddard had. But he did argue in terms that the Revolutionary generation and those seeking developed religious freedom understood. He was John Wise, who was on the other side of the wall from Stoddard, so far as consociation was concerned.

In 1710 his *The Churches Quarrel Espoused* and in 1717 his *Vindication of the Government of New England Churches* argued local autonomy and the power of individual churches over against Presbyterianizing trends among the latter-day Puritans. Decades later Nathanael Emmons was to pick up the logic of Wise's argument: "Associationism leads to Consociationism; Consociationism leads to Presbyterianism; Presbyterianism leads to Episcopacy; Episcopacy leads to Roman Catholicism; and Roman Catholicism is an ultimate fact." This ecclesiastical line of thinking was also to come into play in political resistance to remote and centralized authority.

If Stoddard fought the Mathers, Wise opposed both schools, for both were drifting toward centralization. No wonder that in the 1770's the generally obscure cleric's writings were lifted up for republication. Stay pure, keep power locally, do not tie in too strongly with a central civil government, he kept saying. A Harvard man who came of lowly roots—he was the son of an indentured servant—he had a democrat's instincts. "No taxation without representation" was a phrase of his ninety years before the Revolution. He opposed the burning of witches and favored inoculation against smallpox, here siding with Cotton Mather. For him there was no clash between revelation and reason. It would be unfair to try to see him as a modern, secular man simply because he anticipated some Enlightenment reasoning. His writings are too few to permit careful analysis of the context out of which he argued. Most evidence suggests that he remained reasonably orthodox.

Exceptions like these kept in mind and then put aside, New England Congregationalism was not showing much vitality or innovation as the century began. Cotton Mather's summa, the *Magnalia Christi Americana*, circulated after 1702, provides a window on its worlds. Biased, narrow, provincial, myopic and astigmatic the author may have been. But one telling point survives: he wrote in order to rescue some glories from the fallen or falling Orthodox church of his ancestors. His "Jeremiads"—the characteristic New England way of recalling the good old days and of bewailing the fall—were subtle advertisements for the validity of the New England experience.

"In an age of Jeremiads the *Magnalia Christi Americana* is the greatest Jeremiad of them all," says Peter Gay, no friend of Mather in our own time. "The *Magnalia* told the Puritans what they wanted to hear."

> God himself had cast "a long *series* of preserving and prosperous smiles" on the early settlers of New England, and now that "the enchantments of *this world*" had "caused the rising generation to "neglect the primitive designs and interests of *religion* propounded by their fathers," God was blasting harvests, drowning sailors, burning houses, and filling the air with pestilence. ... Puritan New England was important, its cause just, and its conduct irreproachable.

But to make his case Mather had to engage in coverups; he was not candid; he lied; he hid the truth. Gay: "The *Magnalia* proves the Puritans guilty, and pronounces them innocent." Mather pretends they had consensus where they did not, and must distort his own documents in order to create the illusion. Let Mather move toward modernity, as in his experiments with inoculation; later in life, in 1721, let him loosen up a bit with *The Christian Philosopher*, which Kenneth Murdock over-lavishly describes as proof that he was "far more 'modern' than his times."

If that late book does show him tilting toward awakened evangelicalism ("A PHILOSOPHICAL RELIGION: And yet how *Evangelical!*") and Enlightenment, the century had opened with him in a lower mood. His diary in 1700 saw *"Satan* beginning a terrible Shake unto the Churches of *New England"*; a *"Day of Temptation"* has come, brought by men who are "ignorant, arrogant, obstinate, and full of Malice and Slander," who "fill the Land with *Lyes."* Mather was losing on all fronts, and with him the tired old order declined.

The action seemed to center everywhere but in the secure establishment. Just before the new century, not out in the Connecticut Valley but right up the street in Boston, the Mathers had met their match in the founding of the Brattle Street Church under the tutelage of merchants who through this fourth Boston church widely publicized their alternative way. Here was an urban and unemotional parallel to Stoddardeanism: baptize any one, admit any one who seems serious to communion; don't exact stories of personal religious experience; let the women help choose ministers; acknowledge that congregational polity could be grounded in Nature and Reason—without needing the Word of God.

Two Brattle brothers picked a half-rationalist Harvard man, Benjamin Colman, as pastor, and had him ordained by English Presbyterians, far from the Mathers' reach. Colman's message and the Brattle Street style differed not too much from the Anglican mode of the times. All was reason and benevolence, gentility and manners. Here was a "way of life" religion that tipped no teacups and called for no emotional response. This was a bland and cheerful adapted Calvinism that strained the bounds of Orthodoxy at every point, but with the power of positive thinking and a lilting manner Colman convinced many Bostonians and especially Harvard people that this was the better way—better than those of either orthodoxy or evangelicalism.

Connecticut leaders fought back against some of the liberalizing trends by founding Yale College in 1701 and settling it in 1716 at New Haven. Yale became a hub of new activities. Ministers in the circle that started and supported it were

also instrumental in calling the meeting at Saybrook whence
issued the Saybrook Platform, an ecclesiastical document
that they still had the power to have the General Court enact
into law. The act showed how little faith many people had in
old Congregationalism and in each other. Saybrook's Presbyterian order, its insistence on the Westminster Confession,
and other features demonstrated that a new mechanism was
needed for supervision and loyalty. Eric Hoffer once said that
some orthodoxy is born not so much of the love of truth as of
mutual suspicion. There is just a whiff of that spirit about the
Saybrook occasion. The schism with some Boston theological liberals was growing. For well over a century and a half
Saybrook and its ethos worked to keep Connecticut alert to
the demands of Orthodoxy. But something about it seemed
wrong; was there less trust in people's desire to converge on
common teaching in a time when this had to be at least
casually enforced? Spontaneity was giving way to formalism.

   If a person went against consociation, sanctions were
provided:

> That, if any Pastor & Church doth obstinately refuse a
> due attendance & Conformity to the Determination of
> the Council, that hath Cognizance of the Case, and
> Determineth it as above, after due patience used, they
> shall be reputed guilty of Scandalous Contempt & dealt
> with as the Rule of God's Word in such Case doth
> provide, and the Sentence of Non-Communion shall be
> Declared against such Pastor and Church. And the
> Churches are to approve of the said Sentence, by the
> drawing from the Communion of the Pastor and
> Church, which so refused to be healed.

The Saybrook Platform, a sign and show of strength, was
actually a mark of troubles. So was the arrival of the S.P.G.
after 1701, or the unseating of Increase Mather as President
of Harvard in 1701 along with the refusal of the authorities to
name equally staunch Orthodox folk in his succession.

Worst of all, in the new citadel at Yale as early as 1722 the new President and his brightest colleague defected to the hated Anglican cause.

One last attempt to hold the old synthesis together was the biggest book yet produced in the colonies, Samuel Willard's unread heavyweight *A Complete Body of Divinity*, a tome that reproduced Willard's dull Tuesday lectures, offerings that matched in style his heavy sermons. He had attracted a following at Old South Church and as acting president of Harvard before his death in 1707; it was these admirers that published his book in 1726. They knew that it was out of date by then, but they paid their respects to the symbol.

Willard opposed rationalism and moralism, but gave subtle encouragement to both, first by making the heart's faith seem too dull and secondly by enjoining so much duty upon people. He had no cure for the diseases he discerned, but he did foresee the rationalism and moralism that were to come to characterize the next phase of staid Boston preaching:

> Hence what caution had Gospel ministers in their preaching up of moral duties... If they preach them as to revive the Covenant of Works, to advance the Righteousness of man, and to depreciate the righteousness of Christ, they are far from being the Ministers of Christ.... Nor indeed do I know of anything which doth more threaten the understanding of true Christianity and the bringing in of another Gospel, than the putting of Moral Virtues into legal dress, and without any more ado, to commend them to us as the Graces of our Christian religion.

All but the few revisionists reach for words like "nadir" to describe the depth of Puritan fortunes in the early decades of the century. The churches were reaching few people in fewer classes. Clerics were losing their prestige. Yet faithful pastors still nurtured flocks and prepared hearts. Under the formalism some vital piety remained. When the Great Awakeners came on the scene, they found that some believers had been awake and others had been merely dozing, not dying. Few could argue that no awakening was needed.

PART TWO

The Great Awakening

3

The Surprising Work of God

Surprise was the characteristic response of the leading revivalists and awakeners to their achievements in late colonial America. This surprise was genuine; it had nothing in common with the fake wonder conjured up by later, lesser mass evangelists who manipulated the crowds. The originals were Calvinists who had been trained to leave everything to God, to find Him at least partly inscrutable. They could not know His times and seasons nor could they predict the reactions of His people. They saw themselves as going faithfully about the business of preaching and caring for souls. Little could they know that they were to be effective, that people would convert and become faithful to covenant and church.

George Whitefield, one of the two prime leaders, expressed this surprise early in his career. An Oxford Anglican, influenced by evangelical Calvinist piety, he was astonished first of all at the effects of the Gospel upon himself back in England. Charles, the hymn-writing brother of John Wesley, the Methodist founder, had carefully cultivated Whitefield, regularly lending him books. Henry Scougal's *The Life of God in the Soul of Man* had an especially strong influence. Scougal criticized existing pictures of religion:

Some placing it in the understanding, in orthodox notions and opinions. Others place it in the outward man, in a constant course of external duties and a model

of performances; if they live peaceably with their neigh-
bours, keep a temperate diet, observe the returns of worship, frequenting the church of their closet, and sometimes extend their hands to the relief of the poor, they
think they have sufficiently acquitted themselves.

What was wrong with that? Young Whitefield considered
himself religious and thought all this was true religion.

But certainly Religion is quite another thing ... True
Religion is an Union of the Soul with God, a real participation of the divine nature, the very image of God
drawn upon the Soul, or in the Apostle's phrase, *it is
Christ formed within us.*

Whitefield's awakening had begun. He surprised himself
thenceforth by finding new resolves, new confidence in his
preaching, success in gaining converts, and a call to America.
When some people instantly saw Christ formed in themselves
he wondered, for his own struggles had been long and hard.
But he followed the call to promote such conversions. Later
he was to become very sure of himself, to know exactly what
he was doing. Any professional or any genius—and Whitefield was both—tends eventually to reach such levels of self-
confidence and competence. But his career had been born of
astonishment.

Whitefield's approach was cosmopolitan. He commuted
across the Atlantic thirteen times to 'my little foreign cure'
until it came to be the major scene of his work. He had an
unerring instinct for fulfilling destiny. Colonial America had
produced only five small cities: Charleston, Philadelphia,
New York, Newport, and Boston. He "worked" them all. He
would preach in homes, churches, meeting halls, under the
skies, wherever crowds might gather.

Whitefield's American contemporary, Jonathan Edwards,
was also cosmopolitan and even macrocosmic in outlook,
but he was a provincial in his field of operations. Edwards
succeeded his grandfather, Solomon Stoddard, in a Connecticut Valley pulpit in Massachusetts. At Northampton he
began preaching without intending special effects. We are

told that while he spoke he would lean on his elbow or lose himself in his manuscript or stare at the bell-rope. He was not and did not need to be a shouter. But he, too, was astonished over what followed. In 1734, five years before Whitefield was to reach America, the whole town of Northampton stirred over the conversions in his church. His grandfather had prepared the climate and clientele, though Edwards was not to agree with Stoddard's approach. The grandson inherited a Puritan piety that was anything but cold-hearted and stiff-necked. He had much going for him. But he still did not foresee what was to happen; his people had been very "insensible of the things of religion."

In 1737 he provided a *Faithful Narrative of the Surprising Work of God.* To Benjamin Colman, the Brattle Street moderate in Boston, he wrote:

> This town never was so full of Love, nor so full of Joy, nor so full of distress as it has lately been... I never saw the Christian spirit in Love to Enemies so exemplified, in all my Life as I have seen it within this half-year.

A grapevine or rumor network spread the news of Edwards' local revival as it was later to communicate the excitements associated with Whitefield's travels; soon all the towns along the Connecticut River were full of stirrings.

The awakenings had been a surprise to the first successful awakener on the eighteenth century scene, Theodore Jacobus Frelinghuysen, the Reformed minister and evangelist in the Raritan Valley of New Jersey who reported the Holy Spirit's activities among his people was early as 1726. While they soon caught on to what they were doing and made the most of it, the members of the Tennent family, the New Side Presbyterians of New Jersey and Pennsylvania, were also caught off balance in their years of team work with Frelinghuysen and all through the 1730's. In the Hanover Presbytery in Virginia revivals came as if by spontaneous combustion, and Baptists north and south began to prosper not because they had calculated and assessed a new climate.

Surprise characterized the attitudes of enemies of the

awakenings, of whom there were plenty. The leaders of the Church of England in the southern colonies had tried numbers of styles of nurture within the context of their settled way of life. People simply did not respond. So the clergy leaned back, acquiesced, and then later defended their relaxed ministry. They would read prayer and give homilies, preside at the ordinances of the Church, especially at Baptism and the Lord's Table. They would make worship available and work under, with, and through their vestrymen who, with them, were making Anglicanism an element in the southern Way of Life. What sense could they make of the itinerants who were successful as they countered Episcopal latitudinarianism with narrowness; compromise with strictness; polite reasoning with emotional appeals?

The northern liberals were even more upset and surprised. It would be wrong to portray them as Deist, Unitarian, or fully Arminian in theology—such developments lay far in the future beyond the 1740s. But they were eighteenth century people who were beginning to soften what was left of hard-line Puritan theology and make it palatable to reasonable and reasoning men and women. They were manifestly earnest and faithful in their ministry to their clienteles, and were responsible in the civic order. They, too, had settled for a way of life in which religion had a secure but not obtrusive role. Now itinerants came into their churches or Separatists split out of them—all in opposition to the century's trend toward the use of reason. What went wrong, that the people of a new age should regress to such emotional styles and follow an unrooted ministry?

The Quakers of Pennsylvania made their way between meetinghouse and countinghouse, seeking quiet and gentility. Few of them were even tempted to join the revivalists, but many of them were disconcerted by them. Old Side Presbyterians were too new in America to be really secure yet as colonials, but they were secure in their faith in the Westminster Confessions and the canons of Calvinism. They were bewildered when men and women who shared their faith emotionalized it and challenged the effectiveness of their ministry.

The surprise that greeted the early stages of Awakening before it became a part of revivalists' bags of tricks ("Look, folks, at what the Holy Spirit is working through poor little ineffective old me!") helps support our point that the Awakening, which was half of the two-part eighteenth century revolution in American religion, was largely unintended and accidental. While every sincere minister of the Gospel intends to change people and is purposive about ministry and congregational life, the awakeners were soon to be helping bring in a new age in religion, a new style for which they could have had few models.

The patterns that they had came from dim anticipations in the Christian past and from their contemporary counterparts in Europe. The concepts of conversion, renewal, and the gathering of people into congregations are anything but new in Christian history. Paul, Augustine, and Luther knew celebrated conversions. Whole populations had turned to faith at the behest of missioners or armies. Christians had often before been devout and pious. The awakeners did not lack literature on the warmed heart and the love of God. But for so many centuries this literature had developed in contexts that differed so radically from the American, and its produced or recorded results were so different from what went on in the eighteenth century, that the people of the 1730s had a right to think of what was going on as "Great"—and new.

A better case can be made for precedent not in remote pasts but in recent Europe. In Germany the Lutherans and Reformed alike were gathering as Pietists, orthodox Christians reacting to dogmatism or formalism and nurturing a warmer piety in forms that were congenial to voluntary respondents and not just to those who "go through the motions". Jonathan Edwards was aware of them. In his sermons of 1739 on the *History of Redemption* he included them among the signs of God's continuing providence. Theodore Frelinghuysen, at the beginning of the revival, may have been shaped by these Germans, but today it is believed that Dutch Calvinism had far more to do with his formation. If so, that influence only reinforces the point that eighteenth century Awakenings were international in character, even if they took distinctive shape in various nations.

The Presbyterians recognize precedents or parallels in Scotland. Whitefield and his circle were giving expression to an Anglican evangelicalism that spread in England and Wales. Renewals were also not unknown in Catholicism. Historian Henri Daniel-Rops has called the seventeenth "the Great Century" in France, because of the outbreaks of piety late in that surprising time. These devotionalisms—including even the more extreme Catholic Quietism—paralleled the American doings, though no self-respecting Protestant would have acknowledged this.

For all the influences from the past and elsewhere, the colonial mixture was sufficiently distinctive that we may properly speak as Lawrence Cremin does of a "developing autochthonous evangelicism" among the many faiths on the new continent. It was springing from the colonials' own soil, taking on their character and fitting into and then changing their environment. News of it spread internationally; Wesley's and Whitefield's commuting were evidences of that. But before long, as Edwards liked to point out, the Old World began to look to the new for precedents in experimental and affective religion. The period before had been characterized by scholasticism and settlement in religion; the subsequent period was rationalist. Between the two moments the awakeners trumpeted their changes.

To phrase things that way is to suggest that the Awakening was gossamer and ephemeral, that it lived a glorious butterfly existence and went as it came. The very words about revival and renewal and awakening imply a pendular swing, a rhythm in religion. What waxes wanes again; what flows, ebbs; what awakens returns to rest and slumber. The images and metaphors have all been common in Christian history. And the Great Awakening was, indeed, short lived. Its outer limits might be said to have begun with Frelinghuysen in 1726 or Edwards in 1734; Edwards' excitements died down by around 1738. The Whitefield crowds of 1739 had declined by 1744, after which his opposition grew. The Presbyterian fervors that led to Synodical schism in 1741 receded enough that there could be peace by 1758. Almost no one spoke of revivals after the late 1750s as being anything but local and sporadic.

The Great Awakening, however, did provide a model and a norm for measuring later events. In 1939 or 1941 people knew at once to name the international conflagration World War II and, after 1945, to fear for World War III because a paradigm had been determined in 1914-1918. Americans know how to measure what is a true depression and what is a mere recession after the Great Depression of the 1930's. So the religionists of 1801 knew to call theirs a Second Great Awakening. In 1857-58, the 1870s of Dwight L. Moody, the twentieth century's teens with Billy Sunday or its fifties with Billy Graham people spoke of awakenings or revivals, numbering theirs from the First. Even the efflorescence of non-Christian (Eastern, African, occult) religions in the 1970s coupled with "Jesus" and "Spirit" movements has been reckoned a Fourth Great Awakening by sober historians.

The Great Awakening, like cultural events of its scope, left a sediment that did not disappear. In the time of the nation's bicentennial Hannah Arendt (*New York Review of Books*, June 26, 1975) said:

> ... if History—as distinct from the historians who derive the most heterogeneous lessons from their interpretations of history—has any lessons to teach us, [the] Pythian oracle [that says "those who do not learn the lessons of history are condemned to repeat it"] seems to me

more cryptic and obscure than the notoriously
unreliable prophecies of the Delphic Apollo. I rather believe with Faulkner, "The past is never dead, it is not
even past," and this for the simple reason that the world
we live in at any moment *is* the world of the past; it consists of the monuments and the relics of what has been
done by men for better or worse; its facts are always
what has become (as the Latin origin of the word: *fieri-
factum est* suggests.) In other words, it is quite true that
the past haunts us; it is the past's function to haunt us
who are present and wish to live in the world as it really
is, that is, has *become* what it is now.

A more positive way to put this is in the form that the contemporary British philosopher Ernest Gellner uses when he
speaks of the altered landscape or moraine that follows a
glacial shift. When a society moves like a glacier "over the
hump of transition" to a new stage, to a new approved social
contract—and the Great Awakening is such a hump and its
effects are the new contract—the society lives with its new
symbols for an indefinite period. They make up the landscape. People can subsequently rearrange the boulders, level
this, raise that, alter another thing. The content of the
symbols can change drastically. Unimaginable differences in
content separate today's Oral Roberts from George Whitefield or Norman Vincent Peale from Theodore Frelinghuysen
and drastically different contexts sever the world of Billy
Graham from that of Jonathan Edwards. Yet the later figures
are perceived as being in continuity with the earlier ones.
Their opponents, if they are high-church or liberal or staid,
are the tolerated exceptions, the slightly "less American"
exemplars of religion as a way of life.

Americans, in short, have learned the lessons of the Great
Awakeners and have neither consciously nor unconsciously
rejected the basic features that they pursued in religion or
community-building. A new style of religious social behavior
and practice, a new culture, and new patterns of thought to
legitimate and inspire all of these came into play. Awakening

subsequent to the combination of Continental Pietism-Quietism, English Puritanism-Methodism, and American Awakened-evangelicalism have never been culture wide. They either reproduce the earlier main patterns or are sub-cultural in impact. What Perry Miller said of the story of Edwards' local revivals became true wherever and whenever religion was influential in America:

> One may well ask what makes such a chronicle of frenzy and defeat a 'crisis' in American history. From the point of view of the social historian and still more from that of the sociologist it was a phenomenon of mass behavior, of which poor Mr. Edwards was the deluded victim. No sociologically trained historian will for a moment accept it on Edwards' terms—which were, simply, that it was an outpouring of the Spirit of God upon the land. And so why should we, today, mark it as a turning point in our history, especially since thereafter religious revivals became a part of the American social pattern, while our intellectual life developed, on the whole, apart from these vulgar eruptions? The answer is that *this first occurrence did actually involve all the interests of the community, and the definitions that arose out of it were profoundly decisive and meaningful.* In that perspective Jonathan Edwards, being the most acute definer of the terms on which the revival was conducted and the issues on which it went astray, should be regarded—even by the social historian—as a formulator of propositions that the American society, having been shaken by this experience, was henceforth consciously to observe. [Emphasis mine]

Perhaps Miller's bias as an intellectual historian led him to sneer at students of behavior and social history; perhaps his own scholarship made Awakenings more respectable. In any case, the Great Awakening is slighted and snobbed out much less now than it was when Miller wrote in *America in Crisis* in 1952.

The Great Awakening should not be confused with all the

political or literary changes and revolutions of the following generations. Edwards was no Jefferson and did not aspire to be one. The awakeners were not republicans or democrats or Enlightened *philosophes*. They did not want to break the bounds of the old Protestantism and even of inherited Calvinism. Whitefield clung so fiercely to Calvinist views of election and grace that to his great grief he long had to sever relations with his tutor and friend, John Wesley. Edwards thought he was doing Calvinism its greatest favor and, without people like him, it might not have survived, for he made it more plausible to succeeding generations. But the revivalists were people of their own time, agents of the break-up of scholastic formalism but not true moderns. They did positively alter the outlook of most American religious people of the time—Presbyterian historian Leonard Trinterud estimates that four-fifths of the colonial church-goers were touched and reinforced by its activities—just before the great political changes, and the two kinds of revolution were interconnected. More need not be said.

No one can write more than mere annals or chronicles of the Awakening without having some thesis, some framework for interpretation and narrative. We can understand Edwards' own narrative bias, that "it was simply an outpouring of the Spirit of God upon the land." The historian who cannot understand that, though he or she need not share it, who cannot get inside the mentality of people who thought that way, will never understand awakeners or the Awakening. But few observers would be content merely to reproduce that explanation.

A Hegelian would have a field day, showing that the Awakening was part of a *Zeitgeist*, a spirit of the times, an enveloping question and concern. Otherwise, why did so many people under so many auspices become concerned all at once about their sin and their finitude?

Why did so many occupy themselves with what Emile Durkheim calls "effervescences," out of which new religions are born? Why did they crowd to hear their own ministers or travelling evangelists use "the rhetoric of sensation" on them? Why did they disrupt their churches and congregations, have schisms, engage in doctrinal debates— in an age that gave every evidence of turning simply secular? What inspired the grapevine, the network, the news nexus of words about spiritual outbreaks here and there? The *Zeitgeist* notice is simply a notice and not an explanation. It says that something was going on but does not say why.

If Hegelianism has fallen out of vogue, the Marxian approach to social movements retains power through its stress on economics and class. Of course some class differences were visible in the upsets of the day. Wealthy, static, established orders in religion and politics were on the defensive. It is true that, in retrospect, the Awakenings appealed more to all but elites than they did to elites. But limits to this ideological interpretation also appear at once. Revivalism has been as much the instrument of aspiring middle classes in the bourgeoisie as it ever was the agency for change among backwoods proletariats. In both cases this revolutionary force could look, to the Marxist, like people who need religion as an opium for the masses. The revivals were both urban and rural. They might attract the admiration of educated and influential people even when they did not convert. Thus Benjamin Franklin could not help but enjoy and admire Whitefield.

Alan Heimert severely qualifies the economic historians' approach and refuses to see the Awakening explained "in terms of a diphtheria epidemic, or the land-bank controversies of the 1730s, or even of the declining fertility of the unmanured farmlands of the American backcountry." True, the people of 1740 noticed that those who possessed "a greater measure of this world's goods" were less ready for Awakening than were the "lower classes." But never was the division "a revolt of the backcountry producers from the stringent controls of the mercantile aristocracy."

For Heimert, the more satisfying interpretation holds that "the fundamental post-Awakening division was an intellectual one—one more aesthetic, in fact, than economic or social." H. Richard Niebuhr saw it all as a conflict between those who "saw the reality of an order of being other than that walled and hemmed in existence in which a stale institutional religion and bourgeois rationalism were content to dwell," and those who did not. Heimert's aesthetic theory, vague as it necessarily must seem to those who seek precise definition, rings true to anyone who listens to grounds on which some people even today accept or reject a Billy Graham. "What distinguished Americans, so far as the 'great debate' of the eighteenth century was concerned, was differences not of income but, in substance, of taste."

The Freudians or Eriksonians can and do add their building blocks when they introduce psychological motifs and see colonials in identity crises. The conversion experience and acceptance into an awakened group gave the uprooted an identity, a people to whom they could belong, a sense of purpose, a way past personal crises. Students of anthropology and the history of religion—one here thinks of Jerald C. Brauer picking up motifs from Mircea Eliade—take this a step further and see at least some later Awakenings as the initiation rites that introduce people not only into the church but also into the larger society. Notice: ever since, revivalists have always suggested that when one is converted he or she leaves the culture behind and signs up with God apart from the world. Precisely the opposite happens. One becomes, in the eyes of the majority, somehow more American, more at home in the culture and its ways of behaving and thinking, by being awakened or revived.

The Darwinians take the measure of the revival and employ theories of cultural evolutionism. Take the second law of thermodynamics and apply it to social movements. The system that makes better use of the energy resources of a given environment will tend to prevail at the expense of those that make less efficient use. The established churches, cold and formal, did not meet the tastes and interests of dispersed and lonely people. The revivalists' churches did, and they gained at the expense of others in this "survival of the fittest" game.

Perry Miller's is an intellectual approach, no surprise to any who have read him cited here. "Historians have variously pointed out that the decade of the Awakening, 1740 to 1750, is a watershed in American development. They have difficulty in putting their fingers on just what precisely the transformation was, since there were no revolutionary changes in political institutions." "After 1750 we are in a 'modern period,' whereas before that, and down to the very outburst, the intellectual world is still medieval, scholastic, static, authoritarian." Alan Heimert adds,

> The Awakening, in brief, marked America's final break with the Middle Ages and her entry into a new intellectual age in the church and in society. Out of the Awakening came new ideas—the many propositions that 'American Society, having been shaken by the experience, was henceforth consciously to observe.' The Great Awakening thus stands as a major example of that most elusive of phenomena: a turning point, a 'crisis', in the history of American civilization.

For him, the change in "the American mind" was central. Georges Sorel or Eric Hoffer would take the opposite approach and see in it all signs of the fear and madness of crowds, the yearnings of would-be true believers. José Ortega y Gasset, who had no reason to comment on it, might well have reminded us that the great changes in history do not necessarily come in catalysm and war, in treaty or earthquake, but when the sensitive crown of the human heart tips ever so slightly from despair to hope as it did in the Awakening.

One of the most serious calls for a theory and beginnings of the attempt to provide one comes from William G.

McLoughlin, a notable historian of revivals and awakenings. After citing Erikson, Durkheim, Ernst Troeltsch (on sect versus church), and H. Richard Niebuhr, he says that "the First Great Awakening in America, which everyone recognizes as a crucial turning point in our cultural history, remains enigmatic. Yet some hypothesis must be offered..." One must spot the social purpose served by the Awakening. McLoughlin turns to the Awakening's ideas for a clue. The Awakening was not a breakdown but a redefinition of the dialectic between reason and emotion, order and freedom. This redefinition helped some Americans later to live with both Enlightenment and Evangelicalism, code words for the central ideas in their nation's spiritual history. Both "sides" hold enough in common to make social life possible, and hold enough separately to make it exciting.

McLoughlin also points to the national implications of this first great intercolonial event. A spiritual communion developed which would lead the Christians to work through America for "the advancement of God's Kingdom on earth" through voluntary activism. "Slowly it began to dawn upon the evangelicals in New England and elsewhere in the colonies that soul freedom required freedom from ecclesiastical domination, from political domination, from economic domination. All of this was not clear until the Revolution was won, but the basis existed from 1740," though the political aspects of the Revolution at first "caught the pietists by surprise." The Revolution itself, a "blend of rationalism and evangelicalism, was—as revolutions go—a conservative one." But few doubt that it was a revolution.

The hypotheses can all be jumbled together: the theological-devotional, idealistic, economic, aesthetic, psychological, evolutionary, intellectual, and dialectical approaches here are mere samples. They do not taken together explain the enigma but they all address it, they all give handles to it. To what do they add up? The Great Awakening of the 1740s was a revolution—an evolution so sudden and drastic and far-reaching that no other word well applies—because it succeeded in first challenging, then co-existing with, and finally in many ways replacing the "Religion of the Colonial Way of Life" with the "Religion of the American Way of Life."

The "Way of Life" is an important if informal concept in American religion. It serves to incorporate the many dimensions of culture—social behavior and thought—that give terms and norms to the majority of the people in the society. Because so much of the change occurred in terms of regress to earlier Christian patterns, the Great Awakening might be seen as a conservative revolution, but a revolution it was. In many respects the Pietist-Methodist-Evangelical revolution turned out to have been more radical than the sixteenth century Protestant Reformation. The Reformation had been in many respects what Alfred North Whitehead called a family quarrel of northwest European peoples who still shared similar world-views. But now a new world view was being born, a new ordering of a way of life occurred. Such a change cannot come without drama, contest, an agon, between churches, parties, and people. Their tensions and conflict make up much of the plot of the Great Awakening drama.

4

That Battering Ram against Our Church

The early American settlers had come to transplant and revise old ways of life, not to replace them. Some of them felt that what they possessed in England or on the Continent was itself already perfect and pure. But they were not always free to nurture it in community. So the community moved. Religion was not always a prime factor in the plantation of communities but where it was straightforward transplantation was the dominant idea. Many New Englanders did more repudiating of the old way than others. They wanted to perfect the positive side of church reformation. But they were also content to identify themselves with the persecuted and martyred faithful who in England had been purged and purified through suffering. The Virginians simply took the existing church along with them. The Quakers were agents of change, but they brought a defined Quakerism along. Continental Protestants were either commercial investors, like the Dutch in New Amsterdam, or refugees, as the people from the Palatine or the Salzburgers in Georgia had been.

Most of them settled down at once. Having found community they were content with it. What discontent there was resulted from contemporary lapses from the original ideals and pieties. The religious covenants had had a kind of objective character. Elites dispensed and monitored them. Ministry was "settled." The laity knew its place. The codebooks imparted the necessary learning to buttress the whole. But early in the eighteenth century the syntheses had become static, the fervor was gone, the self-renewing character had disappeared. The Great Awakening, partly unintended and accidental and almost always a surprise, challenged and supplanted the tired earlier settlements. One can tell that a kind of revolution was occurring by noting the suddenness, the consistency, and the inclusiveness of the reactions to it.

Indians, Negroes, and Jews were not threatened. The Indians and Negroes were both a little better off because of the Awakening. Revivals reinspired mission and care and, in many instances, moderate humanitarian ventures toward them. Jews were neither numerous enough nor established enough to be assaulted. The Reformed establishment had already been weakened in New York and it offered little resistance to Frelinguysen in New Jersey. Books on colonial Lutheranism run to scores of pages on these years and hardly mention the Great Awakening favorably or unfavorably. While Michael Schlatter among the Reformed or Henry Melchior Muhlenberg as a Lutheran pioneer were influenced by continental Pietism and were friendly to moderate evangelicalism in the middle colonies, their churches were not entrenched enough to have produced a culture-wide way of life that needed defending. A couple of learned articles deal with Quaker resistance in Philadelphia, but the Quaker establishment was falling without the help of revivalists' battering rams. The German peace sects in the Pennsylvania backcountry had no moats or fortresses that needed defense.

The battles went on in what we have called mainstream religion, the culturally-central and numerically strong groups that "ran the show" and had much to lose through the threat of change. Ezra Stiles's "big three," the Episcopalians, Presbyterians, and Congregationalists, had most to lose.

The Anglican tensions were naturally strongest in the South, where the Episcopalian way of life was entrenched by law and custom and where Episcopalians were soon to lose out in the Westward sweep of migration. Today not a single southern county in any state has more Episcopalians than it has adherents of some other church. Baptists and Methodists dominate in most of them. The Awakening assaults came first from an Anglican, George Whitefield, who essentially did not want to disturb the peace and who at first was welcomed in some Church of England parishes and pulpits. But the good spirit toward him could not last.

We have already seen that the Anglicans did not turn to the Awakening. They were languishing, being invaded by Presbyterians and Baptists and even Lutherans; they were leaving a spiritual vacuum. But they had neither will nor skill to change circumstances. To repeat the quotation from Raymond Albright: "By this time the Great Awakening had come to Virginia with little approval and often open opposition by the Anglicans. Only Devereux Jarratt, who was greatly influenced by George Whitefield, seemed to be touched by the movement." That was late, in the 1760s, and Jarratt was "not bred in the church."

Episcopalians did not partake in the Awakening but they took part in criticism. In South Carolina, Alexander Garden, the Anglicans' commissary, not the noblest in the line of John Blair and Thomas Bray, was custodian of the standing order when Whitefield attacked Charleston for its dilettantism and diversions. Garden tried to keep Episcopalians together. How could Whitefield have taken it upon himself to criticize these ladies and gentlemen "of the first *Figure* and *Character* in the Place?" Pleasures and balls were not the *"Danger to Religion"* or to the *"Peace* and *Happiness"* of Society that Whitefield's *"Mobb-Preachings"* were. And on Garden's terms he was certainly correct.

Why, asked Whitefield, should he respond to Garden's summons and appear in his church courts? Why, he asked, did not Garden's Church return to the Calvinism it was deserting? Why, asked Garden, should so much be made— and here he was right on target in focusing on conversion—

of "the Belief and Expectation of a certain happy *Moment,* when, by the *sole* and *specifick* Work of the *Holy Spirit,* you shall at once (as 'twere by Magic Charm) be matamorphosed?" Whitefield defended the "constant Tenour of my preaching in *America,*" as "*Calvinistical*" in substance—though not in form, for his was Calvinism aimed at the affection and passions, where Garden thought religion ought never be located.

In New England Episcopalianism was a newer force, but it was no less dedicated to order and gentility, to religion as part of a reasonable way of life and not an instrument of the passions or of civil unsettlement. In 1742 Connecticut Anglicans who had themselves been intruders with the S.P.G. in 1701 or upsetters when Timothy Cutler was converted at Yale only twenty years earlier in 1722, found a defender in Cutler's side-kick Samuel Johnson. Johnson noted that the "best of the people of all denominations" feared that "enthusiasts would shortly get the government into their hands and tyrannize over us."

The Episcopalians could treat the New England Awakening two ways. They could join the Congregationalists in criticizing it but could also profit from its presence because they regularly picked up people who reacted against revivalism or tired of the tensions and schisms in the established church. Cutler himself even thought it a good moment in which "every honest Churchman" and "even many sober dissenters do think a resident Bishop would be a blessing." A bishop would help produce order. The New England Episcopal churches all sealed themselves off from Anglican George Whitefield's preaching. Henry Caner at Fairfield spoke for the Episcopal gleaners who profited from the policy:

> Where the late spirit of enthusiasm has most abounded, the Church has received the largest accession. Many of those deluded people having lost themselves in the midst of error, wearied in the pursuit, as their passions sub-

sided, sought for the rest in the bosom and communion of the Church; and others, reflecting upon the weakness of their former dependence, which left them exposed to such violent disorders, having likewise thought proper to take shelter under the wings of the church.

Such whistling did not dispel the darkness. Anglicanism had two-score S.P.G. missionaries making quiet gains in New England, and were never able to team up with the Congregational Standing Order to form a unity against "enthusiasm," which was the age's negative term for religious claims of immediate experience and passion. But Timothy Cutler condensed the way defenders of the settled way of life religion in both churches saw the disturbances:

Whitefield has plagued us with a witness, especially his friends and followers, who are likely to be battered to pieces by that battering ram they had provided against our Church here. It would be an endless attempt to describe that scene of confusion and disturbance occasioned by him; the divisions of families, neighbourhoods, and towns, the contrariety of husbands and wives, the undutifulness of children and servants, the quarrels among the teachers, the disorders of the night, the intermission of labour and business, the neglect of husbandry, and of gathering the harvest. Our presses are for ever teeming with books, our women with bastards; though Regeneration and Conversion is the whole cry... In many conventicles and places of rendezvous there has been chequered work indeed, several preaching and several exhorting at the same time, the rest crying or laughing, yelping, sprawling, fainting; and this revel maintained in some places many days and nights together without intermission; and then there were the blessed outpourings of the spirit. The *New Light* [the name for the revivalists, who expected "new light" from the Spirit] have with some overdone themselves by ranting and blasphemy, and are quite demolished; others have extremely weakened their interest....

Sometimes the newest comers—in this case, the Episcopalians—are the first to utter the Americanism, "Dammit, there goes our neighborhood."

The Reformed and Presbyterian groups, particularly the latter, had not been on the scene long enough to have reason to look established. The Presbyterians, we have seen, were themselves an eighteenth century arrival. Most of them came with the migrations of Scotch-Irish after 1714; yet a quarter of a century later they were already so involved in defense that they had to eject the New Side counterparts to the New Lights in a schism at Synod in 1741—a split that was overcome in a reunion of 1758.

If Whitefield's was a reworked Calvinism within Anglicanism, the Middle Colonies' Awakening theology was also Calvinist. Leonard Trinterud has made the case that few ties can be found connecting Frelinghuysen to German Pietism, but his Dutch enemies did call him bad names of Dutch awakeners. The evangelist never cited German pietists but constantly referred to Dutch evangelicals and Puritan divines. This is important, because it certifies even more that the battle over the Awakening was within the Calvinist house and not between houses in Presbyterianism. Frelinghuysen also got much of his power through linkage with the remarkable Tennent family who disturbed the Presbyterian peace in the Philadelphia area. William Tennent, Sr., William Tennent, Jr., John Tennent, and Gilbert Tennent all joined in their attack on the "presumptuous Security" of their own church members.

John Tennent began revivals at Freehold, New Jersey, but the better-known Gilbert Tennent—who later riled up New England settled pastorates with his sermon of 1740 on *The Danger of an Unconverted Ministry*—had successes around New Brunswick and Staten Island in 1729. Both became friends of Whitefield some years later, but had first established their own pattern. Controversy followed their work, as the subscriptionist party that wanted to enforce assent to the Westminster Confession stood in opposition to the Tennents and the impressive following they were picking up at their Log College, an agency for training new-style ministers. By 1734 the subscriptionists were ready to make a move, demanding supervision over revivalists. They wanted nothing to do with rude ministers trained at the Log College, which was no respectable university. In 1741 the Log College people were driven out—but it was to them that future victories belonged. They changed the face of Presbyterianism and left behind as one of their legacies Princeton University. Long-vacant congregations that would "sign on" a Log College minister were to be guilty of "censurable offenses." The technical name for the minister's fault came to be called an "intrusion." Nothing stopped the intruders, neither censure nor rage. By 1753 the revivalist faction had almost supplanted the older style of scholastic university-oriented, settled Presbyterianism in the north.

In the South, Presbyterianism had an even weaker toehold by the time of the Awakening. But the instinct to settle into the southern way of life's religious patterns was strong. Few wanted to "make waves" or call attention to themselves—as awakeners inevitably did. The Presbyterians could not help notice the enduring attraction of moderate establishment. David Duncan Wallace's History of South Carolina noted a drift from Presbyterian and other dissenting churches to the Anglicans right up to the Awakening:

> The beauty and dignity of its services, the moderation of its conduct, the broad toleration for wide varieties of religious temperament, the agreeableness of its associations, and for a long time the political as well as social advantages that it conferred, all contributed to the steady drift into its fold from among the more wealthy and socially distinguished element of Dissenters.

The South, however, was not to be populated just by

wealthy and socially distinguished people. In the 1740s it was suddenly getting new infusions both from England and from the northern and middle colonies. A new kind of Presbyterian settled, not on the shores and lowlands but in the back country where Whitefieldians, New Light Baptists, and other ministers who were seen as "mechanics and illiterate novices" outnumbered the elites.

In the Virginia valley the Old Side Presbyterians, in power at the time of the schism of 1741, were predominant. But soon William and Gilbert Tennent and other talented evangelists like John and Samuel Blair or Samuel Finley organized churches both in the Valley and in the Piedmont. Then came William "One-eyed" Robinson, an Awakener who stirred Hanover Presbytery in 1743. He directly attacked the establishment. "Unlawful meetings" followed, and revivalists were fined "for impiously and blasphemously reviling our Holy Religion." The governor wanted local authorities "to suppress and prohibit, as far as they could, all itinerant preachers."

Samuel Davies, the greatest of them all, tried to play by the rules. In 1747 he took up work, getting permits eventually for seven pastoral charges. But he was not satisfied with these, and the General Court limited his activities. After raising funds for Princeton in England Davies came back to win new favor as a recruiter of soldiers for the French and Indian War, a patriot, an inhibitor of the more outrageous itinerants, and a converter of some upper class people. These Presbyterians were to play an important part in the American Revolution and the struggles for religious freedom in Virginia.

The Baptists had begun as a despised people, but by Awakening times even they had come to display the beginnings of an establishment. In New England Ezra Stiles made a distinction between the two types, the older Regular Baptists who had blended their way into the environment, and the disruptive Separate Baptists whose Awakened fervor made them "disturbers of the peace." He came to long for the "good old Baptists." William McLoughlin, the historian of these dissenting movements, says that

> to the educated urban Baptists the Awakening seemed an unmitigated disaster for the denomination. It spoiled all hopes for catholic fraternalism with the Congregationalists, it ended the harmonious fellowship among the various persuasions within the denomination, and it lost for the Baptists everywhere the hard-won respect of the influential members of the Standing Order.... But for the growth of the denomination, the Awakening was a godsend.

In the south, the even fewer old-liners came to be called Regular Baptists. They joined Old Side Presbyterians and Old Light Congregationalists and "good old" Baptists as defenders of the old way of life. The Separate Baptist invasion was rather late—Shubal Stearns and Daniel Marshall made their move to Virginia in 1755—but they were immediately visible, embarrassing and successful. The Regulars wisely linked up with the Separates in 1787, asking that party names should be "buried in oblivion."

In New England the contests were most intense and the agon between the Old Light and New Light took on classic and even paradigmatic proportions. The Connecticut Legislature in 1741 was concerned enough to approve a proposal to hold a "General Consociation of the Churches" at public expense to bring peace for "the true interest of vital religion." Ezra Stiles looked back on the "unhappy excesses" of 1740 in *A Discourse on the Christian Union* in 1760:

> In the public mistaken zeal, religion was made to consist in extravagancies and indecencies, which were not according to the faith once delivered. Multitudes were seriously, soberly and solemnly out of their wits.... Sober reason gave way to enthusiasm.... Besides this, the standing ministry were aspersed, and represented under abusive suspicions of being unconverted, legalists,

Arminians. And as they were thus publicly and inde-
cently vilified, so it was taught as a duty to forsake their
ministrations, and form into separate assemblies.
Stiles remained a defender of establishment. He thought that
if the sects were moderate they could balance each other after
"temporary collisions, like the action of acids and alcalies
after a short ebullition" for friendly cohabitation. "The sects
cannot destroy one another, all attempts this way will be
fruitless.... Nothing however will content us but actual experiment—this experiment will be made in one century, and
then perhaps we shall be satisfied." Stiles thought New
England's polity best, "where *congregationalism* is the establishment" without infringing on the essential rights of others.
Such serene faith in harmony was not to prevail in the 1760s
any more than it did when the Awakening had first hit New
England.

The Awakeners attacked unconverted ministers and
half-converted sinners. They itinerated and intruded in
settled parishes. They attacked the intellectualism of Harvard
and Yale and the sterility of spiritual life everywhere. Some
of the invaders were extremists—John Davenport was so er-
ratic that he was later even declared unbalanced—but all
looked extreme because they were disruptive of settled order.
The central confrontation was between Jonathan Edwards
and the best defender of the settled way of life in congregationalism, Boston's Charles Chauncy. Chauncy had himself
tried revivalism, found that he was not effective or that he
did not believe in it or both, and defended reasonable
religion.

Curiously, Chauncy, a rational theologian, an Arminian,
a Unitarian in the making, and by almost anyone's later
definition the liberal over against the evangelical Jonathan
Edwards, found himself speaking for a party called the Old
Side defending the Scripture as if he were a literalist against
the enthusiasts. Do not look, he said, for more New Light
and spiritual illumination; "keep close to the Scripture and

admit of nothing for an impression of the SPIRIT but what agrees with that unerring rule.... The Bible is the grand test by which everything in religion is to be tried." Here is the last-ditch defense for static order in thought:

the Spirit does not lie, as some may be ready to imagine, in giving them new revelations, in suggesting to their tho'ts new truths, which the world knew nothing of before; but in setting those old truths, which are contained in that public, standing, authentic revelation of the divine mind, the holy bible, before their view.

It was the moderns that now looked medieval, the liberals that seemed conservative, the 'radicals' that turned canonical, the democratic thinkers who defended the dying church establishment. The antecedents of today's revivalists and conservative evangelicals were bringing in the new order, the new way of looking at, experiencing, and arranging religious life.

The old way of life religion survived, transformed as evangelicalism was constantly to be. But in neither the eighteenth nor the two later centuries were its assumptions to be attractive to the American majority. One settles or graduates into the Episcopal, mainline Presbyterian, left-over Congregational and even Unitarian or Quaker churches by the deliberate avoidance, often on grounds of taste, as Heimert would have it, of the majority view. Thanks to the Great Awakening the American religious map began to change, to give room for the revivalist churches—Baptist, Methodist, Disciples and Churches of Christ—and the Continental immigrant churches that never shared in the old establishment.

The American religionist, far beyond the borders of Protestantism, ever since has tended to be formally though not substantively evangelical by instinct and reflex. If he is or becomes anything else, such a move appears to be against the stream and the grain. The dimensions of the new order that has brought about this instinctive evangelicalism need to be spelled out, for their bearing on personal, institutional, ecclesiastical, and intellectual life.

5

The Revolutions
of God's Great Design

The Great Awakening was an intercolonial interchurch movement whose complexity elicits the word 'enigma' from historians when they try to account for its outbreaks and forms. No single theory or explanation satisfies. Taken as a whole the Awakening can be seen as an event or a process in the course of which the religion of the colonial way of life was supplanted by a second way—the evangelical route through which, ever since, a person might become a fervent American believer.

Such a movement over a hump of transition characteristically meets resistance and produces conflict. Opponents of the Great Awakening everywhere and almost at once diagnosed with some accuracy what was occurring. On differing theological grounds, settled and serene Anglicans, Congregationalists of the Standing Order, Old Side Presbyterians, Regular Baptists of North and South, and Old Light New Englanders all saw their world threatened. They organized to resist the awakeners. Within a few years the Awakening itself had quieted or passed. But the sediment or residue permanently altered the American spiritual landscape. It remains now to point to some of the dimensions of change. The revival events added up to an unintended and accidental Revolution. Most of its consequences could not have been foreseen by the preachers who concentrated simply on converting souls to Jesus Christ. It was also perceived as a potential revolution by its enemies. Was it a revolution at all?

Historians debate endlessly about the meanings of the term "revolution." They agree that there was a French Revolution, or a Bolshevik or Maoist one. The sounds of guns were not subtle signals announcing revolution. But was there an Industrial Revolution, or was there only an intensification of processes that had been going on for centuries? If a revolution has to imply bloodshed or the absolute alteration of every circumstance of life, the term should not be applied to the Great Awakening. No one was killed, no one forcibly seized power, no one came forward with a ready-made charter for a new order of the ages. And there had been precedents for some aspects of revival and renewal, just as contemporary renewal movements were happening in Europe. But if a revolution can imply a complex of quantitative changes so sudden and far-reaching that they amount to what is experienced as a qualitative change in the circumstances of life, the Great Awakening was a drastic and never repealable event.

First, people recognized changes in the role of the person, the individual, or the self in Western religion. The philosopher Alfred North Whitehead commented on this element chiefly by reference to the Wesleyan-Pietist-Methodist movement. He noted that people of genius in the eighteenth century began to make direct intuitive appeals to the hearts of people. Leaders were less ready to argue, to reason, to engage in constructive theological statement than their predecessors had been. They sensed that a new kind of person who was more free and more self-determining, was emerging. This person needed a different kind of address.

Jonathan Edwards sought a focus in "the affections." Both he and, more readily, his opponents, spoke favorably of "the passions." For Edwards, says Perry Miller, "an idea became not merely a concept but an emotion." Enemies of the Awakening criticized enthusiasm, thus stigmatizing all efforts by evangelists to reach people without making use of logical propositions, without proofs or reasonings about the truth of faith. The Anglican Timothy Cutler knew this in Connecticut, as did Charles Chauncy among the liberal Old Lights or Ezra Stiles among the conciliators. The people knew this. They may have been fascinated by the stormier and more impassioned pitchmen, the Tennents and the Davenports. But Benjamin Franklin is a rather sober witness to the emotive power of the somewhat more staid George Whitefield.

The users of the intuitive approach diagnosed the peoples' hopes and fears and enthralled them with the threat of hell or with the hope of heaven. Timothy Cutler called Gilbert Tennent a "monster! impudent and noisy" for telling his hearers that "they were *damned! damned! damned!* This charmed them..." Chauncy tried to use the scripture against the enthusiastic spirit. In that case the liberal was sounding fundamentalist. He was even forced to show that New Testament times were qualitatively different from those of the present:

> The work of the Spirit is different now from what it was in the first days of Christianity. Men were then favoured with the extraordinary presence of the SPIRIT. He came upon them in miraculous gifts and powers.... But the SPIRIT is not now to be expected in these ways.

Christianity, he said, is "settled in the world." The term is most significant when used by an Old Light establishmentarian.

> ... Christ and his Apostles usually in their preaching addressed themselves to the Reason and Understanding of their hearers: They laid the Matter for Conviction before them in a calm and rational Manner; and thus they treated their hearers as rational creatures; not beginning at first to Work upon their passions and Affections, they used very much Gentleness and Mildness in their preaching.

Both liberal and conservative scholastics lost their

argument with the revivalists. Religion is supposed to be deeply felt. In America the immediate experience is always prime. Anti-intellectuals have the majority on their side ever since the Great Awakening. The effervescence of each revival rapidly passes and becomes routinized. But lip service at least must be given to affective religion. What Whitehead called the appeal to constructive reason in matters of faith has been segregated in some liberal pulpits and seminaries.

New theories or doctrines of man were coming into play in the Awakening. These were wedded to democratic sentiments and emerging psychological understandings, though neither of these were yet to be stated with full appreciation of their political or scientific implications. Alan Heimert and Perry Miller even go so far as to say that "the central conflict of the Awakening was thus not theological but one of opposing theories of the human psychology." Charles Chauncy and his colleagues, who with all their love of science and everything new, became known as antecedents of the liberal Unitarians, defended the old "faculty" psychology. Meanwhile, Edwards, often typed as a forefather of the less intelligent and less progressive breed of revivalists, was the forward-looking antagonist. Having read John Locke's *Essay on Human Understanding*, he was prepared to argue that the human personality was an organic unity. Cognition, knowing, or being reasoned with, were signs of being "affected." Chauncy wanted to control both the imagination and the passions. Edwards connected them with the human whole. Edwards' *Treatise Concerning the Religious Affections*, a classic in religious psychology, countered Chauncy and warded off those Awakeners who dealt only with narcissistic emotional indulgences. He successfully blended the conversion experience with thought and action, and both anticipated the pragmatic style and the learning-through-doing method. "The main and most proper proof of a man's having a heart to do anything, is his doing of it."

If this concept of the person began with an organic psy-

chology and relocated the affections and passions in relation
to reason, a second element of the Awakening had to do with
the decisive religious turn, conversion. Religion that is
"settled in the world," as Chauncy would have it, always
minimizes, makes less of conversions and sudden turnings.
Ernst Troeltsch and his followers have shown how in the
religious arrangement that he called the classic "church"
type, people are simply baptized into the church and thus
into the culture. The "sect" or the disciplined minority group
rescues people from the world through their conversion. In
the revolution that went with the Great Awakening,
Americans began to place a premium on conversion even
when their religious organizations blended dimensions of
both church and sect.

Ever since that time, people like John Williamson Nevin,
who was a High Church Reformed theologian in nineteenth
century Mercersburg, Pennsylvania, have had to push uphill
to prevent conversion from becoming the be-all and end-all
of faith. Nevin's contemporary, Horace Bushnell, a liberal
Congregationalist, wrote *Christian Nurture* to describe an alternative to radical conversionism. His following also knew
that its members swam against all tides. Sam Hill, a historian
of southern religion, argues that conversion is at the center of
everything that happens there. He is correct. But what he
notes is not unique to the South. Whoever reads the literature
of testimony and apology produced by the evangelical
majority cannot but be impressed by its obsessive concern to
elaborate on a moment of conversion. This fascination was
in part a transformation of the Puritan legacy. People were
expected to "own the covenant" and also to have a certifiable
experience of grace. But that experience originally located
them in a static and settled community. The new kind of conversion was supposed to look independent and self-gener-
ating. The rhetoric of the day subtly implied that the convert
could now stand *contra mundi*, against the world, and live
in sovereign independence while at the same time he could

join the larger community, the acceptant American culture that was emerging.

Whether the convert was moved by a Freylinghusen or a Whitefield, a Shubal Stearns or a Jonathan Edwards, he would not likely have been aware of the cosmic context of the experience. Still, such a convert was regarded as someone who should be honored to know that he was standing at the center of the universe. Something ontological was going on in the pews and aisles of Northampton: if I am converted, there will be a different arrangement in the very order of things. I do not simply take my place in a settled order but am an agent of the new things God would work in the whole world.

After a sinner becomes "sensible to" his miserable condition he is thrown upon God's self-initiated mercy in Christ. This leads him to experience the joy of salvation—the joy that Edwards noted in his narrative of surprising conversions. So consistently and so conventionally were these stages in conversion regarded in Great Awakening times that it is hard to recall the fact that in much of Christian history they had not been accented the same way. The revivalist knew very well what these stages were and what part he might play as God's instrument in inducing them. Evangelists had to learn and then employ the "rhetoric of sensation" where once they had simply expounded the verities of dogma and faith.

Few within the movement worried about the effervescences or, as they were then known, the "extravagances" that were evident in these stages. Enemies of the revival did. Friends worried about these only when they were evoked by an unbalanced preacher like the raving itinerant James Davenport. For the most part, however, evangelists could see that most people knew their own bounds. It has always been easy to overplay the emotionalism, thanks to the negative pictures of the critics like Timothy Cutler or Charles Chauncy. If people favor experimental religion, emotion must be permitted some rein. "Our people do not so much need to have their heads stored, as to have their hearts touched," said Edwards.

The combination of the intuitive appeal and the affective response led to a new personal relation to the Church and the Kingdom. H. L. Mencken has spoken of the phrase "to get religion" as an American neologism based on American necessities and priorities. A revival did move a person from latent to patent church membership. The Great Awakening instead implicitly suggested that each person "started from scratch" and, after having entertained other options, chose to respond to the evangelical one. Judaism might be transmitted through the genes and the race. A Jew might choose to attend synagogue or not, but he or she does not choose to be or not to be a Jew. Older Puritanism, even when it allowed for "owning the covenant," still saw continuity in the family. Edmund Morgan says that in a way the faith was passed through the loins of godly parents. But ever since the Great Awakening each new generation must be won, must be converted, just as the lapsed contemporaries of the godly parents have to be reclaimed until they, too, "get religion."

While one hesitates to use the term democratic too casually at this point, it would also be irresponsible to avoid mention of the fact that the Awakening's approach did have a democratizing tendency. Where religion had once been parceled out by elites who were custodians of canons and codes, now the simplest Northampton townsman and backwoods Carolinian were treated as subjects of infinite worth and their affective responses made history. A kind of aristocracy of the converted appeared. Observers have often noted how the Great Awakening contributed to increased lay participation. Lay exhorters were needed simply to keep up with what Edwards called the "business of religion." More than exhortation was involved. The laity were also tutored to become critics of their own clerics, to find new means of Christian expression, to regard religion not as a settled matter but one about which the unlearned could also make intelligent choices.

Historian Richard Bushman summarizes this case:

> The converts of the eighteenth century proceeded with much more boldness than those of the twentieth. Placement in the center of the regnant American theology gave people courage. In the belief that God was with them, obscure men demanded more passionate preaching or a voice in ecclesiastical politics or even the right to preach themselves. Some broke free of their churches; others stayed within and reformed the ecclesiastical structures. In one way or another, they wished to create a new society, beginning with the church, that accorded with a vision of life opened in the Awakening.

Leaders "whose personal and intellectual capacities commanded universal respect" supported the laity. C. C. Goen, a student of the New England Separate Baptists, sees that the "whole movement [was] essentially democratic, and gave a tremendous new importance to the common man." After the revivalists' prime, some new limits were placed on the churchly expression of the laity. But "there remained... a strong deposit of laicism in the churches which owed their renascence if not their origin to the Great Awakening."

If the person was treated as worthy of such status, the Great Awakening also revolutionized religious institutions. Instead of accepting "settled" and "established" ministries—which had characterized Congregational, some Presbyterian, and Anglican ways of life in the 1740s—people, now could set up shop for themselves. Ever since, religious institutions have had more of an *ad hoc* character.

Devastating change came about as a result of the practice of "itinerancy" and "intrusion" on the part of ministers into settled parishes or towns. The Brattle Street Church in Boston first nettled the establishment in this respect. Increase Mather was critical because its minister avoided and evaded the given institutions by being ordained in England. "To say that a *Wandering Levite* who has no Flock is a Pastor, is as good sense as to say, that he who has no Children is a Father."

More than two centuries later it is hard to picture how threatening "intrusion" was to Old Side Presbyterians or "itinerancy" was to Old Light Congregationalists. Americans have subsequently become accustomed to the dislocations brought about by mass mobility and the freedoms that go with religious pluralism. Cooperative churches today may work out elaborate "comity" arrangements to prevent them from stepping all over each other, but they have learned to live with the fact that evangelistic free enterprisers will still invade their territory. Not so in pre-Awakening times, when attempts were still being made to retain the old territorial parish concept that had marked Europe and England for many centuries. Without this pattern, how could there be careful and concerned shepherding of souls? Would not the laity become confused, free or forced to go after the more sensational but probably less faithful and true ministers? Daniel Rogers's case was typical. After Whitefield influenced him he left his Harvard tutor's post, was ordained, and began to itinerate. A Boston newspaper in 1742 editorialized that Rogers would be "a vagrant preacher to the people of God in this land; contrary to the peace of our Lord the King and Head of his Church and to the good order and constitution of the churches in New England as established by the Platform." The Virginians were no less disturbed by Samuel Davies, who somehow could never learn to be content with license to lead seven Presbyterian charges. George Whitefield was an irritant wherever he went.

The civil authorities sided against vagrants and itinerants in ways that they could not after the Awakening and the Revolution. In 1743 Connecticut Governor Jonathan Law defended laws against "Enthusiasm" and "Itineracy." In case London officials might worry about repression here, he explained: "You see Sir in all this there is no Shadow of Imposition but all the Freedom that Heart may wish for." In this case, hardly thirty years before the Revolution, dissenting Deputies in London had to teach the colonies something about religious freedom. Too bad, they said, about revivalist "delusions." But

> ... great and manifest as those Mischiefs are, Wee cannot be of Opinion that, the Magistrate has any thing to do in this matter; but to see that the publick peace is preserved; that there are no Riots or Tumults, and that his Subjects are not allowed to assault, hurt, maim, wound, plunder or kill one another in those Religious Contests.

Small comfort was this to Connecticut officialdom; the itinerants were not guilty of Riots or Tumults, but they were turning the world upside down anyhow. Michael Zuckerman, who has remarked on the pressures for homogenity in New England towns in the eighteenth century, fingered the itinerancy problem, for

> it not only endangered local harmony directly, setting neighbor against neighbor in an effort to 'tell the sheep from the goats,' but also jeopardized it more deeply, in its assault upon the self-containment of the homogeneous congregational unit. Itinerants menaced the local monoliths by introducing competing sources of value into the community...

Such antagonism was "no mere transient tactic" in this conflict. "It was the expression of an endemic, abiding assumption of community organization."

A corollary to the problem of itinerancy and vagrancy was the introduction of the competitive voluntary principle in church life. While full separation of civil and religious realms was later needed to bring this principle to maturity, it was the Great Awakening that, two decades earlier, had established it. European dissenters had sometimes been free to propagate their views without experiencing total repression. In the colonies there had been increasing toleration for the non-established churches. But until mid-eighteenth century

America there remained officially in nine colonies and unofficially in more than these a religious "host culture" which tolerated a number of "guest cultures." But the awakeners were altering all that, moving people toward religious parity, both in the eyes of civil society and in each other's.

If a George Whitefield could draw thousands of Bostonians to his preaching of Anglican Calvinism, what sense did it make to extend all the privileges to the Congregationalist minister who spoke merely to dozens or hundreds? In the middle colonies, the change in attitude was less visible because it was less difficult to bring about there, but bewilderment over the options also grew on that Quaker and Presbyterian soil. In 1759 and 1760 the Reverend Andrew Burnaby catalogued the churches and found

> a good assembly-room belonging to the society of freemasons; and eight or ten places of religious worship; viz. two churches, three quaker meeting-houses, two presbyterian ditto, one Lutheran church, one Dutch Calvinist ditto, one Swedish ditto, one Roman chapel, one anabaptist meeting-house, one Moravian ditto; there is also an academy or college, originally built for a tabernacle for Mr. Whitefield.

How could a settled church ever be official in such a pluralist context? May the best revivalist win! When Presbyterians would divide, as they did in 1741, who could discipline the excluded or schismatic group?

The voluntary and competitive character of the Awakening parallels in its democratic principle the personal appeal of revivals noted above. In famous passages, historian Wesley M. Gewehr, who concentrated on Virginia revivals, spoke of the changes wrought everywhere:

> ... the Great Awakening was one of the secret springs which directed the actions of men, and, therefore, was one of the sources of the democratic movement so closely identified with the American Revolution. The evangelical doctrines ... inculcated ideas of self-govern-

ment... The Church was open to all alike.... Thus we see in the evangelical groups a great leveling influence at work, which could not fail to have important consequences.

The Great Awakening gave rise to popular forms of church government and thus accustomed people to self-government in their religious habits. The alliance of Church and State, the identification of religious with civil institutions, was found to be detrimental to the cause of religion.

... Perhaps unconsciously, but none the less in reality, the Great Awakening gradually welded the common people into a democracy which in the end was to change inevitably the temper, if not the form, of government....

The story of the ways in which ecclesiastical events and adjustments were eventually to impinge on civil affairs is still ahead of us. Gewehr's generalizations are broad-stroked, vulnerable, able to be challenged by monographists at several points. But he was not mistaken about the direction being taken as early as the 1740s. Speaking of Davies and the Presbyterians in Virginia, he also saw a

wider significance than the mere establishment of another group of religionists in the colony. It was a portent of a social and political as well as a religious revolution in the life of the colony—the beginning of a movement from below which was constantly to push upward the common folks to a respectable plane in society and politics. This upheaval began in the church and gained in momentum by reason of the zeal of the leaders, the number of adherents, the popularity and reasonableness of its program...

So far, so good. But all this was not only an event subject to Whig or Marxian interpretations. Wealthy people and lay elites—to say nothing of the most notable theological minds of the generation, like Jonathan Edwards's—were also part of the upheaval or revolution.

Finally, the Great Awakeners forebode or initiated some significant theological alterations. While seen to be divisive, they also had their unitive casts. Across denominational lines people regrouped in the face of evangelists' magnetism. No matter that Whitefield was an Anglican or that the Tennents were Presbyterian; their causes were seen to be linked. Since the Reformation there had been numbers of minor attempts to bring about cooperation across church lines. Some of these were imposed by civil authorities. Some were humanist in outlook. But evangelicalism, with its common interest in the affective heart and not in the fine rules of church order or the precise outlines of dogma, brought people into programmatic and prayerful unity. The common impulse was to break apart in the face of new denominationalisms after the Second Awakening. But from then until now Americans have had some sense that even their fervent anti-liberal religious leaders should be mutually acceptant. If the modern ecumenical movement grew out of some revivalist sources, the revivalist churches that stayed apart from that movement have through the years found it important to make common cause with each other, as they did in the twentieth century by forming a National Association of Evangelicals or by cooperating in ventures like Key 73, an effort to "win a continent to Christ."

The theology of ecumenism came to be complemented and supported by a new set of theories of learning. Richard Hofstadter has stressed that much of evangelicalism was an agent of anti-intellectualism in America because the scores of evangelical colleges were agencies for propagating revival. Evangelicals do have much anti-intellectualism for which to be accountable. Yet the First Great Awakening did also contribute to higher education. Princeton and Dartmouth were but two out of many colleges begun as a result of it. These colleges were started by what today we would call denominations. But in order to enlarge their markets and fulfil their charters, they had to transcend sectarian lines. They were designed to provide new-style ministers, but the

founders also had faith in non-religious subjects. They may
have preferred the less settling styles of the Awakening to the
staid ways of Harvard and Yale, but they would also try to
fuse cognition and affection on Edwardsean psychological
lines.

Theology was not central to the movement, but it was
implicated. Most of the Great Awakening occurred in
Calvinist hands. The Second Great Awakening had more
room for Wesleyan Arminians. It is true that the Whitefield-
Wesley conflict in England was born of their agonies over
these two sets of interpretations. But to their respondents and
hearers, the revivalists' approaches transcended the details of
both schools. The Arminians never forgot God's initiative
and the Calvinists in effect, if not always at first in theory,
gave humans much responsibility. Otherwise, why should
anyone bother to come to revivals; why listen to evangelists?

One theological note that began to come to the fore in the
Great Awakening was to be of great import for the
Revolution, nation building, and later American religion.
Long-overlooked was this most important motif, the millen-
nialism that was to bear on both civil and churchly life.

Christians had always anticipated a Second Coming of
Jesus. In times of plagues and upheavals they might seek it
with fervency. At other times, it was a back-of-the-mind or
end-of-the-church-year idea. In any case, this coming was a
given, part of the settled order, hidden in God's time-table,
unaffected by human concern. The Great Awakening theology took millennial thought and placed it in the front of
peoples' minds. Illiterates, mechanics, farmers, travelling
evangelists, and repentant sinners, were all given a place in
the cosmic scheme. In the conversion appeals hell, not
Armageddon, was used as the threat. More than a century
later 'premillennialism', the idea of a need for rescue from the
world before the sudden Second Coming, was proclaimed.
But in the First Awakening a postmillennial theme dominat-

ed. The change toward Christ's thousand-year rule was to be gradual, and people could participate in bringing it about.

Jonathan Edwards consolidated the vague preachings of others into a whole millennial system. The millenarianism that once led many Calvinists to defeat and dismay was replaced by a sense of joy for sharing with God in his purposes.

God's great design in his works, is doubtless concerning his reasonable creatures, rather than brute beasts and lifeless things. The revolutions by which God's great design is brought to pass, are doubtless chiefly among them, and concern their state, and not the state of things without life or reason.

The human is the measure of all things in the millennial tendency. The change "will not be accomplished at once, as by some miracle" but will *"gradually* [be] brought to pass." The "happy revival of religion" was itself looked to by Edwards and others as a "sign of the times." As the revival waned, Edwards had more difficulty convincing himself and others of that new day's imminence. Liberals like Chauncy could be gloomy about a world of cataclysm and setback, though liberals are often thought of as being the progressives and optimists, and though Edwards's contemporaries typed him as a pessimist. But Edwards could never lose faith in the millennial future, which was to begin to break in to the America of the 1700s:

We are sure this day will come; and we have many reasons to think that it is approaching; from the fulfillment of almost every thing that the prophecies speak of as preceding it, and their having been fulfilled now a long time; and from the general earnest expectations of the church of God, and the best of her ministers and members, and the late extraordinary things that have appeared in the church of God, and appertaining to the state of religion.

The Awakening may have been Great, but people who

thought in these terms saw it as only one of many "signs of the times." Other events still in the future could also be labelled Great and people could look forward to them in hope and joy.

PART THREE

The Revolution

6

Religion and Public Liberty Are Intimately Connected

So far as religious interests were concerned, the American Revolution both preceded and followed the War of Independence. The far-reaching changes in the situation of the churches occurred after 1783. In that period of Constitution-writing and nation-building epochal shifts in the understanding of religious freedom, the distinction between civil and religious realms of life, the voluntary principle in church, and interpretations of the part religion should play in the republic, all occurred.

We know less and are less curious about the details of churches' participation in the war itself. In the writing of American religious history, relative pauses appear in historians' accounts of the years 1775-83, 1861-65, or 1941-45—as if their cameras are in stop-action positions or the churches are in a kind of suspended animation. The reasons for these pauses and interruptions are fairly obvious. War is such an overwhelming preoccupation that most historians instinctively devote themselves to the cannon and treaties when discussing periods of military conflict.

On the home front and away from the scenes of battle in most wars, churches usually go about business as usual or fall into holding patterns. They do not try to resolve the issues that preoccupy them in peace time. Of more interest are periods of the preparation and mind-changing. It is more

worthwhile to watch the American churches of the 1840's
and 1850's debate slavery and disunion than it is later to
follow their wartime chaplains making the rounds, or to
report on their relief work and the devastation their buildings
suffered. So with the American War of Independence. John
Adams' classic text for the idea that the Revolution preceded
the war also applies to the spiritual dimensions.

What do we mean by the Revolution? The war? That
was no part of the Revolution; it was only an effect and
consequence of it. The Revolution was in the minds of
the people, and this was effected, from 1760 to 1775, in
the course of fifteen years before a drop of blood was
shed at Lexington. The records of thirteen legislatures,
the pamphlets, newspapers in all the colonies, ought to
be consulted during that period to ascertain the steps by
which the public opinion was enlightened and informed
concerning the authority of Parliament over the
colonies.

Many of these pamphlets and newspapers also had to do
with the religious agitations and cautions of the period.
Adams gave due credit to these long before he wrote those
famous words to Jefferson in 1815. These public expressions
may give misleading impressions. They may lead to
over-estimations of the part the churches played in the
coming and the prosecution of the War. Most believers who
were patriots were no doubt much like the "Unknown
Citizen" of W. H. Auden's poem: when there was peace, he
was for peace; when there was war, he went, because he
"held the proper opinions for the time of year." Yet those
opinions issue from somewhere. Many of them come from
the influence of the pulpit or the prayer-circle.

The churches' parts in the American Revolution were not
always consistent and calculated. Almost no one, as late as
1765, was saying, in effect: "Let's have a revolution. Let's
separate from repressive old England. Let's start a chain of
decolonializing processes in motion and inaugurate a new

age." The Revolutionary War was brought on by circumstances and emotions. Often it twisted and distorted the purposes of the people on both sides who had helped induce it. For the most part—so far as churches were concerned—its coming was not looked for or planned.

The recently converted members had not become Christian first of all in order to be political. Not a few complained about the preaching of too much politics from the pulpits. Not too many citizens were even in range of pulpits. The church leadership, meanwhile, often worked in the churches' own self-interest. It happened that some of those interests turned out to be supportive of the Revolution or were pieces in the mosaic that made up the Revolution. If clerics provided ideology for war and independence, this came as a spill-over from the energies of people who were reluctant to draw the full consequences of their preachments. When support of the War of Independence was called for, the churches were found to be divided. Their participation was late, reluctantly offered, carefully guarded. Moderate leaders wanted to go back to regular church business as quickly as circumstances permitted. They paid a price for their involvements in any case, because they had been contributing to a society in which political and economic life came increasingly to prevail at the expense of religion.

The story can be exaggerated from two directions. One can concentrate on the War of Independence as a military and diplomatic event, treating religion only in a casual and possibly even negative paragraph. The churches were weak. The aroused people of the day did what they felt they had to do. If religious leaders went along with them, all right. If not, they were left behind. The opposite distortion comes from intellectual historians who, recognizing the contributions of churches to the life of ideas during the shaping of the mind of the colonies overlook the blood and guts, the dollars and bullets, and the day-to-day preoccupations.

Between these extremes, religion can be seen to have had a

significant but apparently diminishing function. Historian Edmund Morgan summarizes the transition that was then in process with considerable accuracy: "In 1740 America's leading intellectuals were clergymen and thought about theology; in 1790 they were statesmen and thought about politics." The Great Awakening was to have social consequences for Revolution and nation building. But that same revival also worked against the inherited ideas of covenant. It had diminished the power and mystique of the lords spiritual in clerical elites and had made religion something of a private affair, a part of individual enterprise. In the process of becoming part of a new way of life, religion had also become escapable in ways that most colonial charterers had never dreamed it would.

Where the churches retained some political power and where their leaders possessed covenants or millennial hopes for the future, they put these to work. But the memories and hopes both varied vastly from group to group. Many faiths in America played such an incidental part in the Revolution that they can safely be overlooked. Churches may have helped sustain citizens through the War years and may have been important to them for some dimensions of life. But the history of popular attitudes for or against King and Parliament or for or against the patriot cause would turn out to be virtually the same whether or not the historical account of churches is taken into consideration. A canvass of some of the religious options reinforces this point.

The American Indians, first of all, were not especially friendly to the British, after the experience of the "French and Indian Wars" only a dozen years before the War of Independence. But they found more reasons later for being with the British than with the Americans. In any case, we know almost nothing of what religious signals were being called one way or the other among these native Americans. In nineteenth century folklore they were linked as cohosts of wartime outlaws in the phrase "Tories and Indians." William H.

Nelson, a historian of *The American Tory* summarizes their stance in one sentence. "The Loyalism of the Indians is well known and contemporary opinion held that the Negroes were dangerously Toryfied." The charge against the Negroes has been qualified through the years as more is learned of their participation in the War, but most of them were not free to do so or say much about what we are here calling the Revolution.

As far as other minorities are concerned, Nelson offers a plausible thesis.

> Among almost all cultural minorities, the proportion of Tories seems to have been clearly higher than among the population at large. The Dutch and Germans seem to have inclined towards supporting the Revolution where they were already anglicized, but not where they had kept their language and separate outlook... Taking all the groups and factions, sects, classes, and inhabitants of regions that seem to have been Tory, they have but on [sic] thing in common: they represented conscious minorities, people who felt weak and threatened.... Almost all the Loyalists were, in one way or another, more afraid of America than they were of Britain.... A theory that the Loyalists were compounded of an assortment of minority groups does not, of course, preclude their having in total constituted a majority of Americans. Without the social and religious homogeneity, without the common purpose, and without the organic and efficient leadership of the revolutionists, the Loyalists might still have outnumbered them.

Nelson allowed for two significant exceptions to this thesis. "The Catholics and Jews apparently form an exception to the rule that religious minorities leaned toward Toryism... It is possible that the Jews and Catholics were in such suspect and habitual minority, that they felt obliged to follow what seemed majority opinion for their own safety." Whatever the motives, most Jews were indeed with the colonials—we know the names of only a few prominent Jewish Tory families. But, with the possible exception of a Haym Salomon or two, the contribution of a minority as small as Judaism was to be insignificant. The stories of the Revolution and the War are virtually the same with or without Jews.

Catholics had little more opportunity. They may have numbered only about 25,000 out of a population of 2,500,000 in 1775 or even as low as 20,000 out of 3,000,000. After one had deducted for laggard and lapsed, aged and infirm, infant and child Catholics, the able-bodied and witted Catholic men and women who might be agents of Revolutionary thought or action number only several thousand. Catholics' role has often been debated. In 1874 the historian George Bancroft charged the Catholics with having been deserters or with never having been involved, while church historian John Gilmary Shea, two years later, argued that there had been no Catholic Tories and that all the Catholic people had lined up with the Revolutionaries. The truth lies between these. There were certainly few public Tories among Catholics, even though one could picture good reasons for Catholics to be disaffected with their Protestant neighbors even more than with Protestant England.

They suffered inconvenience and repression on all sides. Their ears could ring with the consistent anti-papal and anti-Catholic rhetoric as Revolutionary issues developed. Thus Samuel Davies in Virginia in 1755 drummed up soldiers for anti-French causes by picturing "our Fellow Subjects on the Frontier murdered with all the horrid acts of Indian and Popish Torture." Could Virginia exchange "her liberty, her Religion, and her All, for arbitrary Gallic Power and for Popish Slavery, Tyranny, and Massacre"? When Heathen Savages and French Papists get together, "the Powers of Hell make a Third Party." No person should let his estates fall "a Prey to greedy Vultures, Indians, Priests, Friers [sic]." "Ignorance, Superstition, Idolatry, Tyranny over Conscience, Massacre, Fire and Sword, and all the Mischief beyond Expression with which Popery is pregnant were threats."

Liberal Congregationalist Jonathan Mayhew told Harvard collegians in 1765 that Rome was "a most corrupt one, a filthy prostitute, who hath forsaken her first love and is become indeed, the mother of harlots." Political leaders were just as uncivil. "I did verily believe and I do so still, that much more is to be dreaded from the growth of popery in America, than from the Stamp Act or any other acts destructive of civil rights." Catholics did have their defenders at times. George Washington let it be known that soldiers who celebrated Guy Fawkes day, an anti-Catholic festival, exercised the worst kind of taste. After the War he gave Catholics his seal of approval. In Maryland and Pennsylvania, their only reasonable strongholds, Catholics had given strong support to the patriots. But the war story comes out virtually the same with or without them. Only one cleric, John Carroll, took an active part. He did so reluctantly as part of a legation to Canada after the Quebec Act of 1774 led some colonists to try to seek Canadian support. It was Carroll who best saw that the War of Independence was not the most dramatic Revolution of the day: "In the United States our religious system has undergone a revolution, if possible, more extraordinary than our political one."

A number of groups in the minority can almost be described as bystanders, so blurry are the lines of their divisions and so casual their choices as war approached. Among these is the relatively large Lutheran confession. Lutheran historians, like heirs of other minority groups from those days, like to certify their true Americanism by pointing to the fact that at each important turn in early American life they were near the center of things. Some few "Old Lutherans," especially if they spoke no English and had adapted little to American standards, were British loyalists. The War was an inconveniencing moment in their church life. They fought in it, taking their turn dutifully in the military. After the repeal of the Stamp Act patriarch Henry Melchior Muhlenberg even allowed himself to be political enough to have a prayer of thanks. But that act was a far cry from true anti-British agitation while the tax was still in force. Lutherans have regularly been passive and quietist in political affairs. They were so consistently trained to be docile and to support "the powers that be" that they could not be counted on to develop on their own the ideas of the Revolution. Characteristically, when the War was over and a new legitimacy had been established they were as loyal to it as they had been to the system it had replaced. In short, they made good patriot followers but leadership among them was rare.

Where the German and Dutch Reformed had not Anglicized, they were not very enthusiastic Sons of Liberty or colonial fire-eaters either. In New York the congregations where Dutch was spoken were almost entirely Tory while the English-speaking parish was more pro-American. At New Rochelle the French Calvinists won praise from the British, but the adapted and blended-in earlier arrivals from French Reformed churches were militantly on the side of the colonies. By this time Methodists were coming on the scene. John Wesley, of course, was a High Church Tory and an enthusiastic one. But he was far away in England, and had little authority over the largely autochthonous and lay-led American church that was forming in the two decades before 1784. If Wesley was an embarrassment in America, Francis Asbury, the first great American Methodist leader, filled the void and helped people forget the embarrassment. Still, many Methodist loyalists had to flee to Canada. In no case are they needed for the telling of a story about how America came to Revolution.

Even more complicated is the career of the middle colony churches that opposed war, any war, and that had to retreat from colonial support as calls for violence grew and killing began. Foremost among these were the Quakers. Now and then they could link up with their neighbors in criticism of

England. Thus Philadelphia merchants opposed the Stamp Act—one is tempted to say, "of course." But the Quakers were surprisingly Lutheran-like in their submissiveness to authority. They derived their approach from the same letters of St. Paul that their Lutheran neighbors did.

They did not want to over-endow government with importance. But if there must be government, let it be that of "the powers that be," which are ordained of God—and they happened to be British. In 1775 the Philadelphia Yearly Meeting corresponded with other Quakers, quoting the Bible and urging them "constantly to remember, that to fear God, honour the King, and do good to all men, is our indispensable duty." Let nothing break our "happy connexion" with England. We should not set up governments and most certainly should not "plot and contrive the ruin or overturn of any of them." No wonder the lapsed and by then anti-Quaker Tom Paine could speak of the "factional and fractional" Tory Quakers. "What more can we say of ye than that a religious Quaker is a valuable character and a political Quaker a real Jesuit."

Quakers exercised discipline against those who refused to take conscientious objector status. Except for a few breakaway "Free Quakers," who took up arms, those who were overtly sympathetic were considered backsliders. They all lived with agony over the problem of paying taxes for support of the war. Some turned anti-government in these years when they finally and almost utterly lost political power in Pennsylvania. Naturally, many of them came to have high regard for the causes of their American neighbors, but they could not contribute directly to Revolutionary ideology. At war's end some loyalists trekked to Canada. The survivors in America quickly adapted to the new "powers that be," authorities that they had done little to help bring to power.

The other peace churches, most of them foreign-language speaking, had similar careers. The Moravians suffered much,

perhaps more than Quakers, for their convictions, partly because they carried on work among the hated Indians even
during the War. Some Mennonites acted as teamsters or
helped the violent cause in numbers of other non-violent
ways. But they could not or should not take up arms in the
War of Independence, and little that they or the Dunkers or
Amish said could be construed as a direct contribution to the
Revolutionary cause. The contentious junior Christopher
Saur at Germantown, Pennsylvania, refused oaths of
allegiance and opposed the war. He found his press destroyed
and was himself persecuted. Peter Brock calls the roll of all
the conscientious objectors and absolute pacifist groups:
"Quakers and closely related groups like the Rogerenes,
Nicholites, and Shakers or... the German-speaking sectaries
of Mennonite, Amish, Dunker, Schwenkfelder, or Moravian
persuasion." This substantial middle colony cluster was in
the midst of a Revolution, but their contributions were
nothing but accidental and unintended.

Thus the members of a majority of religious groups were
reluctant or resistant Revolutionaries. But *not* the larger
number of congregations. In 1780 there were over 1900 congregations of Congregational-Presbyterian-Baptist persuasion, whence much Revolutionary talk and action came, or
of Episcopalianism, which was a divided church. This total
should be compared to a mere 624 Reformed-Lutheran-
Catholic local churches, many of them very small. After the
reluctant patriots and the largely Loyal churches are sub-
tracted, we are once again left with the "big three" that we
met under Ezra Stiles's tutelage. Now it is enlarged to include
the several hundred newer Baptist churches, most of them
offspring of Congregationalism, that he had not chosen to
notice in 1783. Their role in this story tells us something very
important about the Revolution. Here is the obverse of the
Nelson thesis about cultural minorities. Majorities provided
Revolutionary thoughts and impulses. With the exception of
Baptist dissenters, who still derived much from the context of

the established churches against which they had begun to rebel, those who supported the Revolution had the biggest stake in the national life independent of England and rich in the promise of colonial liberties. Members of these churches spoke not as dissenters at all but as defenders of a new order already emerging and under their control.

Significant differences existed within these churches, of course. Just as large minorities and perhaps even majorities of the general population were in the "neutral or opposed" category as the War broke out, so were the church members in the population. Episcopalians were sorely divided. In the northern colonies, in New England or New Jersey or New York, most of them sided with England. Yet three fourths of the signers of the Declaration of Independence, it should be remembered, were Episcopalian laymen. Pro-Revolutionary Episcopalianism, then, was the established church of the South and not the dissenting church of the North. It was the church that had much to lose if the Americans lost, and that had something to gain if they succeeded.

The Episcopal contribution in the southern states, however, hardly ever came from gifted and articulate clerics. It issued from those responsibly relaxed latitudinarian and Arminian vestrymen who drew more on their own practical wisdom, on Greece and Rome, on Locke and Harrington than they ever did on Cranmer and Hooker and Anglican divinity. Their story belongs more to that of the rise of the "religion of the Republic" and has less to do with conventional Episcopalianism.

Samuel Seabury, soon after the war to become the first American bishop, stated the case for Loyalism. If one was devoted to the Church of England, he was inevitably connected to the Establishment and thus to the Crown. Seabury bet on Order, in a statement to the Society for the Propagation of the Gospel during some pre-war violence:

I think that even these disturbances will be attended with some advantage to the interest of the Church. The usefulness and truth of her doctrines, with regard to civil government, appear more evident from those disorders...

... the more candid and reasonable people... seem heartily tired with the late clamours for liberty, etc., as it appears evident that unbounded licentiousness in manners, and insecurity to private property, must be the unavoidable consequence of some late measures...

Prominent clerics like Jacob Duché of Philadelphia's Christ Church—who switched sides, having been chaplain at the opening of the Continental Congress session in 1774—or Charles Inglis of New York's Trinity Church also spoke up for England. Since such leadership was not matched on the other side by clerics or theologians in the Church of England—no matter how many Episcopalians were with the American troops—it cannot be said that the emerging church in any way intended a Revolution. It was the sons of a dying style of Episcopalian network who helped speak up for independence.

Those who observe an elimination process in my accounting can find that not only were the more or less established "churches of the majority" the speakers for Revolution but now, with Episcopalianism largely set aside, all that remain are the three that were most directly involved in the Great Awakening of the 1740s—the Congregational-Presbyterian-Baptist nexus. Their connection is by no means accidental. These were the main ecclesiastical instigators of thought in support of the Revolution that John Adams said had occurred from 1760-1775. Joseph Galloway, a Loyalist who testified before Parliament after leaving Pennsylvania, said that the opponents of the British Government in 1774 were "Congregationalists, Presbyterians and smugglers." Read "Baptists" for smugglers, in religious translation, for they smuggled in Baptist causes in Revolutionary rhetoric and then turned out to be supporting Revolution while defending their Baptist causes.

A notable chronicler of this fact on the English side was
Edmund Burke, who in his *Speech on Conciliation with
America* in Parliament on March 22, 1775, did some enumer-
ating:

> ... Religion, always a principle of energy, in this new
> people is no way worn out or impaired; and their mode
> of professing it is also one main cause of this free spirit.
> The people are Protestants, and of that kind which is the
> most adverse to all implicit submission of mind and
> opinion. This is a persuasion not only favourable to lib-
> erty, but built upon it.... the dissenting interests have
> sprung up in direct opposition to all the ordinary powers
> of the world, and could justify that opposition only on a
> strong claim to natural liberty.... All Protestantism,
> even the most cold and passive, is a sort of dissent. But
> the religion most prevalent in our Northern Colonies is a
> refinement on the principle of resistance; it is the dissi-
> dence of dissent, and the protestantism of the Protestant
> religion. This religion, under a variety of denominations
> agreeing in nothing but in the communion of the spirit of
> liberty, is predominant in most of the Northern Provi-
> inces, where the Church of England, notwithstanding its
> legal rights, is in reality no more than a sort of private
> sect...

Burke vastly overstated the character of their dissent, but
properly located the impulses for religious change. These had
all been awakened churches. Thus they combined some intercolonial, interdenominational sense, a feeling for a growing
national identity, some millennial instincts about the
American theatre of God's new drama, a regard for
individual responsibility, a faith in the way passion and
reason could be linked, a distrust of elites, and a willingness
to forget about old hierarchies and status-systems. If the
Awakening had made religion a private matter, its leaders
also saw public consequences develop from it. Thus when
Jonathan Edwards as early as 1747 asked for a Concert of

Prayer to oppose "infidelity, heresy and vice" he linked up with clerics in Scotland to seek "an express *agreement*, unitedly to pray to God in an extraordinary manner, that he would... *pour out his spirit, revive his work*, and advance his spiritual *kingdom* in the world, as he promised." Edwards thought this should go on "till *whole nations* be awakened."

Whole nations: this is fresh language, still more religious than political, but not without bearing on the political concerns that were soon to come. Each group took up the concerns in different ways. The Presbyterians were divided, in part on ethnic lines—though these should not be overdramatized. It happened that the Scots dragged their feet in the hill country of North Carolina or even on the southern coasts, while the Scotch-Irish caused some enemies to call the events of the 1770s "a Presbyterian War." Tories were generally rare in this Church. New York's Chief Justice William Smith and his Pennsylvania counterpart William Allen were prominent and rare Presbyterian Loyalists.

In Mecklenburg County, North Carolina, some Scotch-Irish people met in the spring of 1775 and spoke vigorously against England—so much so that some Mecklenburgers to this day claim (on the basis of dubious documentation) that they had declared independence at Charlotte more than a year before anyone else did. A better claim of fame issues from Hanover County, Virginia, where on October 24, 1776 the Presbytery became the first ecclesiastical group in America to identify with the Declaration of Independence and its causes: "...your memorialists are governed by the same sentiments which have inspired the United States of America: and are determined that nothing in our power and influence shall be wanting to give success to their common cause."

Samuel Davies had been so militant already in 1759 that he could say that "the art of War becomes a Part of our Religion" against the French. The Protestant British-American combination then fighting Catholic France was seen to be an agent of "the commencement of [the] grand decisive conflict between the Lamb and the beast," and would help usher in *"a new heaven and a new earth."* This millennial language the Presbyterians conveniently used against the British a few years later. The foremost Presbyterian spokesman became John Witherspoon, who came to America in 1768. Of him and his kind Elias Boudinot, a third noteworthy anti-Revolutionary Presbyterian layman, was to complain in 1776:

> Our clergy unhappily have gone distracted, and have done us more injury than I am afraid they will do us good, in a great while. They have verified what our Enemies have so often prognosticated. We have been quarreling with the Ch. of England these 40 years past, about uniting Civil and Ecclesiastical Power, and now at the moment we have the shadow of Power in our Hands, we are running into the same extreme... This has given amazing offence and has raised a cry agt our clergy that must ruin their influence in every station.

Patriots, of course, were not offended by this emerging Presbyterian majority that linked up with New England clergy in pre-Revolutionary thinking.

The Baptist case offers some exceptions and differences. Here were chiefly New England Congregationalist Separatists, products and agents of The Great Awakening, and pietists of sorts whose concerns were not really concentrated on establishments and politics, on interests of this world and the social scheme. Yet in order for them to survive and prosper, they had to make their way against the Congregational Establishment. In the southern colonies their agents teamed with Thomas Jefferson, James Madison, George Mason, and other Episcopal laymen against Episcopal establishment. In the north they first sided with the Crown, almost until 1775, in order to find freedom against the Congregational establishment; at that time they acted the part of the weak minority group.

None of their instincts made it possible for the Baptists to remain in such an alliance. They were to find that their anti-Congregational arguments made more sense against England itself. Isaac Backus, their leader, signifies these turns, but he had company in James Manning, the president of the new Brown University at Providence, and other Baptist spokesmen. Their ire rose over the Stamp Act and over rumors of attempts to seat an Episcopal bishop in America. In his history in 1784 he listed the Episcopal threat as the greatest cause of Revolution. Significantly, in 1763 he had been as concerned about Congregationalist tyranny. "For my part, I am not able to get a pair of scales sufficient to weigh those two great bodies in, the Episcopal hierarchy and the New England Presbyterians [he meant Congregationalists] so as to find out exactly which is the heaviest."

After weighing all Backus' unconvincing arguments in his own scale, historian William McLoughlin summarizes the case:

> The truth is that the Baptists of New England were undecided about which side to choose until almost the last minute; some of them in the more remote areas of New England, were never wholeheartedly behind the revolt. When, in 1775, they were forced to make a choice, *most of them discovered almost by impulse that they were with the patriots.* But it was not a choice which they had helped to create. The Revolution caught them by surprise. They produced rationalizations for patriotism after the fact. As dissenters, rebels against the system, outsiders, they had not shared in the making of colonial policy and had not been called upon to ask themselves what really was at stake from 1765 to 1775. [Emphasis mine]

McLoughlin resisted the familiar notions that they were patriots because they believed in the priesthood of all believers and of the sacredness of conscience. The neutral and Tory churches also believed this Great Awakening background of individualist, experimental piety was of help to them—but it had to go through many transformations and was the victim of numerous contingencies and accidents along the way.

The establishment, the makers of the system, the insiders, the Congregational-Presbyterians of New England, were only partially caught by surprise. They have always been the subjects of greatest interest when religious Revolution in America is mentioned. They were old, powerful, well-situated, revitalized by the Awakening, infused with new rational thought. The Old Light (now "Liberal") ministers conventionally preached Election and Fast Day sermons. These were leatherbound and preserved as marks of their importance. While Liberal clerics' status was declining relatively, they still cut a figure in their communities. The New Light, Awakened, or Evangelical Calvinists had overtaken them in numbers and were in new situations of power. Together they made up what the Tory Peter Oliver called "the black Regiment." They talked and wrote much, but Oliver blamed them for more than words. They

> were also set to Work, to preach up Manufactures in-
> stead of Gospel—they preached about it & about it, un-
> till the Women & Children, both within Doors & with-
> out, set their Spinning Wheel a whirling in Defiance of
> Great Britain: the female Spinners kept on spinning for 6
> Days of the Week; & on the seventh, the Parsons took
> their Turns, & spun out their Prayers & Sermons to a
> long Thread of Politics, & to much better Profit than the
> other Spinners; for they generally cloathed the Parson
> and his Family with the Produce of their Labor—this
> was a new Species of Enthusiasm, & might be justly
> termed, the Enthusiasm of the Spinning Wheel.

The course of the Black Regiment toward Revolutionary engagement was wayward, fragmented, full of inner contradictions. It is difficult to tell the story without endless qualifications, finger-crossings, "on the other hands", and ambiguities. New England had its Tory clerics, too. Many other ministers and lay leaders saw religion as something not of this world, and made no comment. Countless clerics wavered, reversed themselves, shifted allegiances with changing events. Almost none walked arrow-straight directions toward Revolution.

As one illustration, the established leaders did not know what to make of Backus and his complaining Baptists. The Congregationalists really thought that their own establishment of religion was so rational, so fair, so superior to all other polities, that dissent should have no reason to complain. On October 14, 1774, Backus and other Baptist delegates met at Carpenter's Hall in Philadelphia. They challenged the Massachusetts delegates at Continental Congress because the means by "which liberty in general is now beheld" did not square with treatment of Baptists in Massachusetts. John Adams tried to defend establishment by showing that it was gentle; "the establishment of religion in Massachusetts is so mild that it can hardly be called an establishment at all." Thirty years later Adams had not recovered from the encounter of 1774, which he neither understood nor responded to adequately.

How, asked Backus, can the established Congregationalists complain about taxation without representation when they tax dissent without giving them representation? They name themselves "*Sons of* Liberty, but they treat me like *sons of* VIOLENCE." Bernard Bailyn reports: "The establishment was shocked; disbelieving." Andrew Eliot, a liberal-minded man, wrote Thomas Hollis in 1771:

> Our Baptist brethren all at once complain of grievous persecutions in the Massachusetts! These complaints were never heard of till we saw them in the public prints. It was a great surprise when we saw them, as we had not heard that the laws in force were not satisfactory... I do not like anything that looks like an establishment.... There is nothing in the present complexion of this country that looks like persecution. Both magistrates and

ministers are as free from it as they ever were in any age or country. If it were not so, I should detest New England as much as now I love it, and if possible would leave it... I hate every species of persecution, and cannot bear that a people should be accused of it that in my conscience I believe are free from it.

Clearly, different assumptions about freedom were in the minds of many Baptists and Congregationalists. Nor were Congregationalists really agreed among themselves. The Evangelicals and Liberals despised each other and agreed on little. But during the years before the War they had much in common and papered over some differences. They were at least coming to a sense of political unity, but tensions often showed. Thus Charles Chauncy, the old foe of the Great Awakening, attacked the Evangelicals because "the Cares of Religion now, in a great Measure, supersede the Affairs of the World." Enthusiasm, in short, rose out of idleness and laziness. The Liberals believed in the "Puritan ethic" more than the more-Puritan Evangelicals evidently did!" Chauncy and his kind most feared their Evangelical counterparts because if they deserted the old faculty theology, "it can't be but People should run into Disorders" and there would be irregularities. This is hardly the language of someone who will be called upon to support the armed violence of revolution, a Liberal who typically was more concerned to see restraints placed on people out of power than on those in power.

Despite grave differences, however, Evangelicals and Liberals could unite first against popish France and the Indians and then against the Stamp Act-era British. They could learn surprisingly to blend spiritual and temporal concerns. Samuel Adams in 1772 noted that the "Religion and public liberty of a People are intimately connected." They rise and fall together. The liberals had long known this and Evangelicals were more ready than before to say this.

The millennial thought of the Great Awakening made this

bond possible. Millennialism is a long-overlooked note in the religion and politics of that day. Earlier millenarian thought had usually been cataclysmic and apocalyptic. It expected a sudden, drastic, painful end of things for Christ's Second Coming. Thanks most of all to Jonathan Edwards and the people who had influenced him, the shift was made to a non-cataclysmic millennialism. The change toward a new order now would be gradual. Christians would be its human agents. Great Britain and France could not possibly be God's final agents—but America could take its place among "whole nations" to complete redemption. Details of contemporary life were interpreted in this scheme. A kind of optimism resulted.

The political reorientation that went with this millennialism was considerable. As Edwards had to show, redemption would no longer be looked for from the time-honored East but from the West. The "latter-day glory" was to begin in America. The old pictures of America as a Zion, an Israel, a city upon a hill were revived and transformed for the new heaven and new earth that were to be devised here. For Edwards the millennium was chiefly connected with piety and awakening, but the concept could easily be politicized and connected with the imagery of national destiny. The good society was on its way. There was no room for pessimism or despair.

At this point pious and Enlightened ideas could meet, so the two schools of thought could employ one kind of futurist imagery while seeking separate goals: a Christian America or a republican America. Both were part of a common "pursuit of happiness." This meant also that America could be interpreted as Israel; its enemies were referred to as Egypt, Pharaoh, Antichrist. In 1781 Joseph Huntington of Hartford pointed to delicious parallels and coincidences between old and new. "The tribe of Joseph was subdivided and became two tribes, *i.e.*, the tribe of Ephraim and the tribe of Manasseh, which made *thirteen united, free and independent states.* "Pride went with the identification. Samuel Sherwood told a Connecticut congregation in 1776: "God Almighty, with all the powers of heaven, are on our side. Great numbers of angels, no doubt, are encamping round our coast, for our defence and protection. Michael stands ready, with all the artillery of heaven, to encounter the dragon, and to vanquish this black host." On this scale differences between Old and New Lights, Evangelicals and Liberals, shaded into mere nuances. For this the Evangelicals were probably more responsible than the outnumbered Boston Liberals. The Great Awakening was past; in 1745 its pickings were already thin. Revivals now were brief, spasmodic, local, quickly forgotten. But the millennium was already fixed in the minds of the preachers. If it was not to come through revival, what would be its substance? The political order came increasingly into view to fill the void.

Between 1758 and 1763 France served as the Antichrist. The anti-Catholicism of the day united the New England parties; it came from so many political and religious leaders, with such consistent use of vitriol, that no purpose would now be served to quote it. In these years a new Anglophilia developed, as the King and Parliament were lauded for their opposition to the pope and his legions; the Glorious Revolution had been the only needed revolution.

Then, just as suddenly, loyalties had to shift when England imposed a Stamp Act. The Liberals were more conservative here, suspecting a "Frenchified" party for perverting pure England. The Evangelicals went further, and began to see England as Assyria itself, swooping down to deprive colonials of liberties. When the Stamp Act was repealed, it was the Liberals who more quickly slunk back to praise England. They were more frightened by the radicalism and anarchy implied by the Sons of Liberty than by a country that had imposed and then repealed an odious tax.

More enduring than the Stamp Act crisis was that induced by the intensification of rumors that the Episcopalians wanted to settle a bishop in America. An S.P.G. agent, East Apthorp, foolishly built a pretentious home at the edge of the Harvard campus. It did not look like a missioner's hut but an Episcopal palace. Jonathan Mayhew, known for his outspokenness, took on Apthorp, the Bishop, and England. Few events did more to stimulate national unity than did this threat. "If bishops were speedily to be sent to America," wrote Mayhew "it seems not wholly improbable, from what we hear of the *unusual* tenor of some late Parliamentary acts and bills for raising money on the poor colonies *without their consent*, that provisions might be made for the support of these bishops, if not of all the Church clergy, also in the *same way.*" Religion and politics were mingled.

It is true that the time had come for a bishop; the church had grown beyond the decent bounds allowed by its almost congregational polity in America. But Bishop Thomas Secker of Oxford knew the problem. "We... must wait for more favourable times.... So long as [dissenters] are uneasy, and remonstrate, regard will be paid for them and their friends here by our ministers of state." More embarrassing: even Virginia and Pennsylvania Episcopalians made clear that they wanted no bishop. No matter; the rumors of one's coming sufficed to quicken anti-British talk.

A third catalyst was the Quebec Act of 1774, which combined colonial fears of Catholicism with hatreds of England in one event. In June, 1774, Parliament enacted the measure that gave the Canadian French the right to exercise their faith and had ceded Western lands to Quebec. The colonists would now be blocked in North and West. The Continental Congress spoke in milder language than did the New England Clergy. It told the British people that Americans could not be enraged over the fact that England should establish in America a faith which "has deluged your island in blood, and dispersed impiety, bigotry, persecution, murder and rebellion through every part of the world."

The Stamp Act, Episcopal Bishops, Quebec Act—these all served to bring together the New England parties, be they religious or secular, into a more united front. The Liberals were more reluctant to make a break. They always feared anarchy. They usually receive the better press among Whig historians because as early as 1750 some of them—Jonathan Mayhew, supremely—were giving discourses against unlimited submission to government. More recently, revisionists have qualified their support. They show that Liberals more often than not spoke up for the propertied interests of their Boston members and were careful not to see liberties extended further. They were hard to like, snobbish about the rustics who had not gone to Harvard, careful to keep their crowd together, critical of the populists and the evangelicals who dealt with the passions. But there is no reason to take away from their own contributions to the language of rights and liberty. What is important is to see the bigger role of the New Lights, the Awakeners turned political millennialists.

The religious Revolution in the black regiments before the War of Independence resulted from a subtle but important change in models, images, or paradigms. Thomas Kuhn's familiar picture of paradigms in scientific revolutions can be applied here. One critic calls these paradigms a "disciplinary matrix," which consists of "the entire constellation of beliefs, values, techniques, and so on shared by the members of a given community." They are also "exemplars," which means "complete puzzle-solutions which, employed as models or examples, can replace explicit rules as a basis for the solution of... remaining puzzles."

When Backus and the Baptists took the language of opposition to church establishment and directed it against British tyranny; when the successors of Edwards translated millennial awakening language to the civil order; when Liberal ministers used philosophical language of rights and liberties; when Presbyterians transformed language of obeying God rather than man to the advocacy of civil disobedience and rebellion, shifts were visible in both the concepts of community and the life of its exemplars.

Somewhere along the way in the 1760s and early 1770s significant colonists tilted ever so slightly toward ideas of liberty and independence. They took their available religious language and used this to legitimate acts of rebellion, war, and nation-building. The nation and its churches were again going over what Ernest Gellner calls a "hump of transition" to a new approved social contract. After the war only a few Loyalists fled. Others changed their positions. Neutrals became fervent American nationalists. The Revolutionary thinkers found their early advocacies of the American Way vindicated, their status secure.

The Revolution came about on many grounds. Some believers reasoned their way into it; more were surprised by it. In most cases churches simply sought their self-interest and found that it linked up with the interest of the nation that was coming into being. They paid a price in a new secularization of thought and style, in their having helped set an agenda in which the established churches would eventually play a less public role. They were not as ready as before to preach jeremiads to themselves, to repent, to rely on grace and not on their efforts. But they had known the excitements and rewards of sharing in what they believed to be a further unfolding of the work of redemption, the spread of God's "latter-day glory" in their nation, their world.

7

Religion Is Divided into Natural and Revealed

The eighteenth century "faith of our fathers" shaped its sons and daughters in two general ways. First, it helped assure that Americans were to be typically and instinctively evangelical in their formal religion, no matter what their church may be. With few exceptions, the norms of the Great Awakening prevail in the judgments made about religious choice. People must "get religion," make a personal decision, become part of a cell of the renewed. Religion must be deeply felt; the "affections" are more important than the intellect. Nurture and reflection are secondary to experience and experiment.

Just as they are intuitively evangelical so are they also reflexively republican and—if this does not sound too contradictory—"reasonable" about their informal religion. Evangelicalism is their focused, concentrated, intentional religious style. Reasonableness is their generalized, diffuse, inevitable style. People who think about and take pains with their faith—including many non-Protestants—show the Great Awakening's influence. The same people also fall back on or share space with others who can rely on the support of the republic's religion. That second faith is a heritage of the late eighteenth century.

The generalizations about typicality and reflexiveness do and ought to leave readers uneasy. Illustrations of how these appear and what they achieve should provide reassurance. As one contemporary example: a fervent Southern Baptist or a member of almost any other overtly evangelical church will normally say that religion is a private affair, a subject of personal choice. This evangelical will be in the front ranks of those who do not want their minister to meddle in politics or to have the government interfere in church affairs. He or she will be a watchdog at "the wall of separation of church and state," to see that no one confuses the two realms. Substantively, this person will tend to be an exclusivist in religion. Salvation is to be known only in the name of Jesus Christ. All other ways leave one at best "half safe" and probably outside the sphere of the good.

The same person will also join a million other people in signing a petition for a "School Prayer Amendment." The evangelical more often than not would like the United States Constitution amended so that public institutions can be scenes of meditation, devotion, Bible reading, and prayer. From his or her clerical leadership will come complaints that the courts have "taken God out of public life" and have done something very unAmerican. How can this be and remain what it has always been, a nation "under God?" It is pointed out to such people that in a pluralist America not every faith can be given equal time in public observances. Therefore, the religion of the schools and public institutions will have to be very general and inclusive. They register no shock. Yet, we might ask them, how can a prayer "to whom it may concern" be effectual if only prayer in Christ is prescribed and effective? How can moral values be taught through a vague religion if Baptist Sunday Schools say that only the grace of God and the imitation of Christ are sure patterns?

These questions do not evoke either bewilderment or angered response. F. Scott Fitzgerald once said that it is the mark of a first rate intelligence to be able to live with two contradictory ideas and still function. Americans have, in that case, revealed astonishing collective intelligence. Sidney

E. Mead once remarked that Americans are in many ways both heirs of Pietism and the Enlightenment. So far as the Enlightenment is concerned, they cherish its practices, but do not know what to do about its theories. His "gastroontological" metaphor was colorful: Enlightenment or rationalist theories rest uneasily in the American's stomach. He is unable to digest them and unwilling to regurgitate them. American life is full of paradox and contradiction, and this particular ability to live with apparent religious incompatibilities is an example.

In the middle of the twentieth century a classic fulfilment of public expectations occurred in the case of President Dwight David Eisenhower, a popular and esteemed public figure. Few chief executives have more frequently or more fervently spoken up for the values of a general, national religion. Mr. Eisenhower did not care at all for dogma or ritual. But he did think that religion had to be very deeply felt and it had to be productive of morals. On those terms he began to fuse his eighteenth century legacies. Still, something was missing. It turned out that just as he had never been a member of a political party, so he had never joined a church. During the presidential campaign of 1952, therefore, he was baptized and owned up to Presbyterian membership. That "therefore" is not written to indicate that he acted in bad faith, only to show how a public could be satisfied. But from the citizens' point of view, only his general and not his focal faith had been taken care of in his public profession. He was an unfinished product in evangelicalized America until he "got religion" personally and particularly.

These events and examples seem far removed from the world of the eighteenth century, but they are not. They show a working out of problems faced in the revolutions of that period. The Great Awakening just before mid-century was the turning point for personal, focused religion. But the third quarter of the same century complemented and then completed the revolution. Sidney E. Mead was correct in his emphatic judgment: "The Revolutionary Epoch is the hinge upon which the history of Christianity in America really turns." In it a "strange coalition of rationalist and pietist" emerged. Mead turns from this statement almost instantly to attend to the pietists' renewed attack against rationalists, an attack that belongs to the Second Great Awakening and the nineteenth century's concerns. But the "hinge" point and the coalitional issue remain.

Not everyone either then or now favored the coalescences and coalitions of that century's contradictory theologies and philosophies. To one side, the Awakening seemed anachronistic, off-schedule on the world-historical time-table. In an earlier chapter we have already heard a rationalist of today scolding or ruing Jonathan Edwards for failing to keep step with Europe's changes. Peter Gay wrote that "in the midst of the greatest revolution in the European mind since Christianity had overwhelmed paganism, Edwards serenely reaffirmed the faith of his fathers." Ever after, in Europe people had to made clearer choices between the revolution in thought and the faith of the fathers. Ideologues there pronounced the death of God and produced pitiless and persistent revivals to historic faith, whose confessors had to take the defense. In America the tension certainly increased between the two. The acts of commuting between them and "plural belonging" to both of them awakens no surprise and produces little confusion in American's minds.

The coalition had been intended or sought, little more than the Awakening's revolution in religious ways of life had been. It seems to have been a by-product, a society's automatic refutation of philosophers' impulse to neatness, a way of muddling through where clear outlines and maps failed people. The pietists certainly disagreed with the rationalists on the decisive issues of life, on matters having to do with what Paul Tillich called "ultimate concern." And the rationalists, far less eager than the European *philosophes* had been to "crush the infamy" of the church and inherited religion, were not impressed by exclusivism and particularity, by "superstition and priestcraft," by revealed religion. They thought these would all tend to fade away in the march of progress, the unfolding of nature, the use of reason. Yet they had to settle for coalescences and coexistences.

No good name for this second party in the eighteenth century religious revolution has satisfied everyone. To speak of the Enlightenment and of Enlightened religion is to adopt European terms and to imply a harshness or militancy about traditional faith that was rare in the American versions. The name "republican" is fairly appropriate insofar as the public dimensions of the faith are concerned, but other dimensions are present as well, and the word republican has become partisan in the course of two centuries. We have used Mead's word rationalist, but the "ist" implies more ideology than it should. The new faith combined John Locke's word "reasonableness" with Thomas Jefferson's concern for the "natural." Whatever term is used, it should not carry connotations of clear definition, partisan neatness, or extreme militancy.

This reasonable and natural faith did not survive intact, untransformed through the decades any more than did the evangelical styles as they were appropriated and changed in black Protestantism, suburban synagogue affiliating, or in the activity of Catholic missioners who met people at the boats and helped them awaken to the demands and joys of religion. Eighteenth century rational religion was eighteenth century rational religion, occurring in an episode with a beginning and an end. It left behind no church, unless one wishes to consider Unitarianism a partial embodiment of some of its impulses. Historic Unitarianism among the churches has the best claims on this faith. But because of the idea that "my own mind is my temple" or that the civil society itself was the sanctuary of this faith, it did not need the "middle man" represented by organized religion.

From some points of view the rational confession was as

much a philosophy as a religion. Yet one would be hard-pressed to find a university philosophy department anywhere in America that teaches this philosophy as a plausible accounting of reality or a respectable pattern of problem-solving approaches. Many subsequent schools of philosophy or literature in America—pragmatism, naturalism, new rationalisms, and the like—have been respectful of the old faith in nature and reason, but they have not drawn on it. The historians are more fascinated than the philosophers; the statesmen have put it more to use than the scholars. As a formal expression it was overwhelmed by the new pietisms of the Second Great Awakening with its revivals. Or it was transformed almost beyond recognition in the romantic national faiths of the nineteenth century. Yet it lives on in presidential inaugural addresses, the rituals of the Boy Scouts and the Public Schools, the rhetoric of the Supreme Court, and in other reflections on the legal tradition, on buttons and bumper-stickers, and in folkloric comment about the equal validity of all faiths insofar as they contribute to morality and the relative irrelevance of each on everything else.

This episode, only a few decades in duration, seemed to be exactly what was needed at the time of intercolonial stress and opportunity, colonial crisis, and nation-building. The people of that day might have spoken of a "providential congruity" between the nation's need and this response. Nature had produced a void and nature filled it. Reason located a vacuum and reason filled it. Certainly the heated-up competitive sects of the Great Awakening, had they been left to their own heritages and impulses, could not have come up with such a blanket faith. For that reason, even without its own churches or schools, movements or institutions, this impulse lives on as a kind of official solution to the national problem. It was part of the moraine left behind when America went over what has been called its "hump of transition" to an approved and enduringly plausible social contract. Citizens will more readily invoke its symbols than apply them or transform its content than reject it, simply because they do not know what the social order would look like were they repudiated and because they represent a satisfying past solution. Subsequent revolutions in American life have not begun by reference to the faith of Jefferson and Franklin and Washington and then been followed with a messianic sort of word: It is written, *but I say unto you.*" Instead—and here I am borrowing an insight from Max Weber and his latter-day disciple Michael Hill—change comes about when the virtuoso looks at eighteenth century faith and says, "It is written, *and I insist.*"

The coalition and coalescence did not come out of two parties totally at war who had nothing at all in common. Pietists and rationalists did not make up armed and isolated camps in the eighteenth century. Communication of any sort seems impossible between people who sense no involvement or shared assumptions with each other. They have to begin with a common humanity, a perception of mutual need and interest, some joint set of memories and hopes. And in this "hinge" or "hump" period they had plenty of these.

Participants in both the Awakening and the development of reasonable religion were part of an *oikoumene*, an international community of impulses and ideas. Of course, they Americanized their appropriations, were not overly influenced by details of Europe's parallel careers, and produced distinctive accents. But they did not cut themselves off from a nurturing larger community. As Edwards was aware of the German pietists and Whitefield commuted; as Methodism took rise from British Wesleyan stirrings and Frelinghuysen was associated with Dutch Calvinist revivals, so were the advocates of reasonable and natural religion in touch with larger currents. Isaac Newton's concepts of order and of God as a moral governor were taken for granted. John Locke as author of *The Reasonableness of Christianity*, a republican theorist, and a contributor to "human understanding" was regularly invoked as were Harrington on politics, the milder

Deists who had made their mark in England by the 1720s, or the Arminians of the Church of England.

Both sides endorsed experience. Edwards, a devoted reader of Locke, argued for an organic view of the person just as Franklin and Jefferson did. Both parties contributed to the pragmatism in American thought. Naturalists and revivalists were both empiricists of sorts, both wanting to check ideas in sense experience. The competitive revivalists spoke for "Concerts of Prayer" and linked up across what became denominational lines, just as the reasonable religionists warred against sectarian boundaries.

Despite internal varieties in each camp and despite overt competition between them, examples abound of appreciations between the camps. Jonathan Edwards' passion for John Locke was matched by Benjamin Franklin's friendliness for George Whitefield. Thomas Jefferson and James Madison may have been outraged by religious establishments and dogmatism. But they were congenial to sectarian advocates of religious freedom and joined forces with these less "reasonable" Christians over against Liberal theologians who clung to privilege and establishment. Both sides rejected old establishments and old scholasticisms. There were learned people in both camps; the "reasonable" philosophy was not technically demanding and did not issue in a grand tradition of scholarship. And the revivalist camp in the person of Jonathan Edwards had one of the finest minds of the century. Both factions respected the Bible, "true" Christianity, and the figure of Jesus.

Reasonable or natural religion on American soil did not, for that matter, grow up entirely independent of the churches. While it was eventually to be reposed in the anti-revivalist parties of the Old Light Arminians and the Episcopalians, it was not even entirely excluded from the Awakening groups. The two religious elements interacted throughout the century during their quests for new ways to relate experience to reason, and sensibility or passion or affection to speculation and idea.

At the beginning of the century Boston's Brattle Street liberals and their minister, Benjamin Colman, began to question irrational or scholastic supernaturalism. But their irritant, Cotton Mather, also at least glimmered some reasonableness in his *The Christian Philosopher* in 1725 and cherished scientific experiment enough to share in dangerous and dreaded smallpox inoculations. Early in the century John Wise, "up from Calvinism" and not yet a true modern rationalist spoke the new language. The idea that "reason is congenate with [man's] nature, wherein by a law immutable, enstampt upon his frame, God has provided a rule for men in all their actions" was teamed with the proposition that "revelation is nature's law in a fairer and brighter edition."

As for the Episcopalians, Samuel Johnson, Timothy Cutler's Yale colleague and partner in conversion, was uttering anti-Calvinistic sounds in the 1720s, saying he had been "much embarrassed with the rigid Calvinistical notions in which he had been bred," and was acknowledging that he had read Arminian divines at Yale after 1714. Johnson was wily enough not to identify himself with the name Arminius, the hated enemy of Calvinists; he only held to Church of England doctrines, but "if *Arminius* happened to agree with them in some of his notions, I know no reason, however, why we should be called after his name."

One hesitates to enter the controversy over the degree to which Jonathan Edwards might be considered a modern celebrator of reason. It is safe to take refuge in the notion that he should be seen somewhere between Peter Gay's picture of him as a medieval man and Perry Miller's too enthusiastic portrayal of Edwards as a Lockean, to whom Christian supernaturalism almost seemed to be secondary and even residual. "Edwards was infinitely more than a theologian." He was a psychologist and a poet, "the child of genius in this civilization." Out of touch with his own day, he speaks "so much ahead of his time that our own can hardly be said to have caught up with him." He was to Miller a kind of empiricist who in 1717 as a fourteen year old had read Locke with more pleasure "than the most greedy miser finds, when gathering up handfuls of silver and gold, from some newly discovered treasure." "He maneuvered a revolt by substituting for seventeenth-century legalisms the brute language of eighteenth-century physics. He cast off habits of mind formed in feudalism, and entered abruptly into modernity.... Without openly proclaiming a revolution, Edwards effectively staged one." "No matter how much [Edwards] called the new simple idea supernatural, the suspicion then and now is that he meant only that it was not unnatural."

Seeds of the second eighteenth century revolution were certainly present in Edwards, but they had developed far less than Miller contended they had. Edwards's *A History of the Work of Redemption*, the book that so enthralled and enraged Peter Gay, shows that his frank supernaturalism and anti-Arminianism kept him from being the prime agent of this turn, however much he may have contributed to modern theories of sensation within evangelicalism. Better to say that he illustrates the ferment, the unrest, the torment of change in his day. To remember, as Gay reminds us, that Edwards was the contemporary or near-contemporary of Hume and Montesquieu, Condillac and Voltaire and even of Gibbon is to indicate how out of line he was with Enlightened thought. A delicious irony for anti-Edwardseans: their anti-hero is read while many of the rationalists and atheists of his time are not, and may have a direct influence far beyond theirs.

The movement of reasonableness and naturalism in religion in what had been the Calvinist camp continued beyond Edwards. Justice Paul Dudley's endowed Dudleian Lectures at Harvard after 1751 were to deal with natural and revealed religion and were to bring to public notice both Calvinist and Arminian contributions. Ezra Stiles at Yale, after having passed through a skeptical period and having duly noticed the comings and goings of Arminianism and Deism, was a reasonable Christian. So was the Presbyterian John Witherspoon at Princeton. A reader of Montesquieu, a common sense philosopher, a radical of sorts who influenced other "founding fathers" just as he was one himself, showed how far the bounds could be pushed. The breakthrough came around Boston among the Old Lights who were turning Arminian on the way to Unitarianism. Their names mean little to most Americans today, though Ebenezer Gay (the only one born in the seventeenth century), Lemuel Briant, Charles Chauncy, and Jonathan Mayhew have probably received a somewhat better press than they deserved. Whenever historians of religion write in embarrassment over enthusiasm and emotion in religion, the intellectual Whigs among them go scouring the past for respectable antecedents, men and women of intellect and reason who might add dignity to their story. In that view, the Boston Liberals look good. From time to time they must also suffer from reactions against that good press. In Alan Heimert's version they were elitists and snobs, provincial Harvard anti-populists who appealed to their merchant clienteles and touted the virtues of privilege and establishment. All that may be true, but they do deserve notice as participants from within the churches in the other half of the century's religious revolution.

In 1726 Cotton Mather could still say "I cannot learn, That among all the Pastors of Two Hundred Churches, there is one Arminian: much less an Arian, or a Gentilist." All were still orthodox Calvinists in the heritage of Westminster and Savoy. Eight years later Jonathan Edwards, with probably equal accuracy, said that around 1734 "began the great noise that was in this part of the country, about Arminianism, which seemed to appear with a very threatening aspect upon the interest of religion here." By mid-century Jonathan Mayhew had become openly Arminian. The chapter titles in Conrad Wright's *The Beginnings of Unitarianism* accurately convey the movement of this school's energies and thoughts. First its members attacked Original Sin, a key to Great Awakening and New Light preaching and thought. Reasonable people knew that a good God would not hold people responsible for Adam's fault. They followed this with attacks on predestination and defenses of "the Freedom of the Will." Justification by Faith, a key Protestant teaching, was scrutinized next. Liberals did not want to be so unProtestant as to teach justification by works, but they saw a complementarity and stressed natural morality.

By 1755 they were frankly setting reason at the side of revelation in defense of rationalism. The doctrine of God had to be treated eventually, and they did this through witness to "The Benevolence of the Deity" and universalism, "The Salvation of All Men" after 1763. The Anti-Trinitarianism that eventually gave them the party name Unitarian logically followed and put them in association with Jefferson and others who thought that Trinitarianism was a daemonism, an atheism. Finally, they defended the Right of Private Judgment over against any idea that the corporate Christian community should shape one's faith.

Those titles and strophes are cold condensations of once warmly debated controversies. One must savor Arminians' own statements. Ebenezer Gay, the oldest of them, took his turn with the Dudleian Lecture at Harvard in 1759. "Religion is divided into natural and revealed:—*Revealed* Religion, is that which God hath made known to Men by the immediate Inspiration of his Spirit, the Declarations of his Mouth, and Instructions of his Prophets: *Natural*, that which bare Reason discovers and dictates." Revealed religion was still the higher of the two, but as years passed and in different hands it came to look more and more supplemental—since human government and institutions had to hold people responsible who might not accept revelation.

Jonathan Mayhew introduced the characteristic eighteenth century language of "happiness."

> As the natural and moral world are under one and the same common direction of government; so God's end in all things, however various and diverse, is really one

and uniform... and tend to the same point at last; the moral perfection and happiness of the creatures capable of it, or the glory of God; which, in any good and intelligent sense, seems to amount to the same thing.

Mayhew may have been the most radical of all. In John Adams he had a press agent who later listed the minister among the half dozen most notable articulators of Revolutionary ideas. Mayhew was so controversial already by the time of his ordination that ever after he was under suspicion. He also regularly revealed how respectable religious New England was. In 1763 he still could say, "there is no such monster as an *Atheist* known amongst us; hardly any such person as a *Deist.*" But to the New Lights and scholastics alike Mayhew himself was in the halfway house to such infidelities.

Men are naturally endowed with faculties proper for distinguishing betwixt truth and error, right and wrong.... Let us retain a suitable sense of the dignity of our nature.... It is principally on account of our reason, that we are said to have been *created in the image of God.*

The vain *Enthusiasts* are "enlightened Ideots" when they forget this and speak of carnal or blind human states. As Mayhew left Trinitarianism and was accused of Arianism, the ancient heresy that downgraded Jesus, he said that "My views are misrepresented." He had not been "depreciating and did not lower the character and merits of Jesus Christ." "I believe in him as my inspired teacher and Savior; my soul loves and adores him." Alden Bradford, his scrupulous biographer, adds a gloss. On this point, "I cannot but observe, that he is not altogether so clear and definite as on most other subjects."

Charles Chauncy, Jonathan Edwards' foe, had the bully pulpit of Boston's First Church for a sixty year ministry during which he could elaborate on these views. No Deist and not even willing to call himself an Arminian, Chauncy spoke the language of reason while defending the old established way of faith. "As the First Cause of all things is infinitely benevolent, 'tis not easy to conceive, that he should bring mankind into existence, unless he intended to make them finally happy."

Only a few churches were thus infected or liberated in the eighteenth century and Unitarianism never became statistically impressive. The Arminians interest the intellectual historians more than they do the social historians, so circumscribed was their influence. But they did serve as one kind of bridge to non-ecclesiastical reasonableness in religion.

Overt post-Christianity in America, by which we mean religious philosophy that was respectful of "true" Christianity but wanted to move beyond its particularity, came late. Orthodox defenders of the Standing Order, always out looking for infidels, looked back on the French and Indian Wars to spot the intrusion of thought that simply could not have represented native growth. A moderate worrier, Ezra Stiles, wrote a friend in 1759 about the links between morality and skepticism in the new thought:

> I imagine the American Morals & Religion were never in so much danger as from our Concern with the Europeans in the present War. They put on indeed in their public Conduct the Mark of public Virtue—and the Officers endeavor to restrain the vices of the private Soldiery while on Duty. But I take it the Religion of the Army is Infidelity & Gratification of the appetites....
> They propagate in a genteel & insensible Manner the most corrupting and debauching Principles of Behavior. It is doubted by many Officers if in fact the Soul survives the Body—but if it does, they ridicule the notion of moral accountableness, Rewards & Punishments in another life...
> I look upon it that our Officers are in danger of being corrupted with vicious principles, & many of them I doubt not will in the End of the War come home minute philosophers initiated in the polite Mysteries & vitiated

morals of Deism. And this will have an unhappy Effect on a sudden to spread Deism or at least Skepticism thro' these Colonies. And I make no doubt, instead of the Controversies of Orthodoxy & Heresy, we shall soon be called to the defense of the Gospel itself.

Deism, the doctrine most people feared but many already held, reduced all religion to several ideas. These included the belief that there is one principle or governor of the universe, a being called God. His creatures, despite his remoteness and lack of definition, were implanted with a moral faculty that made it possible for them to live a virtuous life. At some time there would be rewards and punishments. The moderates said that revealed or particular religion could supplement these basic tenets. The more consistent and radical Deists saw historic and revealed religion to stand in its way. French thought, which enjoyed a minor vogue after the treaty of 1763 (but which was almost wholly repudiated thirty years later when the French Revolution took offensive turns) was more skeptical and naturalist.

Only a few Americans ever signed up in the radical camp. Ethan Allen wrote the first book that was overtly critical of religion in the colonies. But he was a better military leader than philosopher, a country bumpkin without intellectual influence. Thomas Paine, ex-Quaker turned Deist, constantly had to fight off charges that he was an atheist. He spoke eloquently of The Age of Reason and has slightly more philosophical influence, but he also misjudged the climate of readiness in the colonies. Elihu Palmer and a few other "infidels" tried to start Temples of Reason in New York; "Illuminati" were spotted in Boston; Freemasons were sometimes considered to be subversive of old Christianity and agents of new reason. Late imports like the chemist Joseph Priestley after 1794 took the new Enlightened course. But the only pattern that had any chance of succeeding and which did succeed in the "hinge period," issued from the very people known as the Founding Fathers of the Republic.

These statesmen who represented their separate colonies had differing reputations in the various colonies. Thus Thomas Jefferson, widely acceptable in the South, was soon to be regarded with great suspicion by New England Federalists of many Protestant stripes, while Benjamin Franklin remained a friendlier figure to all but a Presbyterian faction that he derided. John Adams had more impact on reasonable religion in New England than anywhere else. George Washington was seen as the father among the fathers, and knew nearly universal acclaim. Together these did not intend a revolution in religious thought. Only Jefferson among them had ideas worth reading later on the substance of religion, though all of them made ingenious contributions to the institutionalizations of religious freedom and to solving some problems of tolerance and pluralism. They were not a homogenous group in close contact with each other all the time. Few of them would have seen their efforts to have a theological tone or bent. Not all would even have thought of their work as religious, so much did they associate religion with dogma and ritual, priestcraft and institutionalism. But in retrospect some clear outlines emerge.

First, to a man, they held at least nominal ties to English Protestant churches. Only Charles Carroll among Catholics wrestled prominently with republican themes. Continental Protestantism was unrepresented among those remembered as natural or republican religionists. The "reasonable" leaders all remained respectful of Christian faiths at their best. That is, they could be extremely critical, as Jefferson was, of what they thought were departures from the pure intentions of Jesus and the founders. But they were also patient with minor flaws and did not only judge Christianity on the basis of its worst expressions.

They were reasonably informed about the Bible and some of their language was shaped by it, though here they had moved far from the biblical expressions of the earlier set of founding fathers, the Bradfords and Winthrops and Penns.

Nor were they as biblically explicit as Abraham Lincoln would be after a century of evangelicalism's influence. They fused this biblical language with talk about nature and reason. Thus a student of Washington's religion has listed his names for God. Few of them were biblical: Supreme Being, Providence, Heaven, God, Grand Architect, Governor of the Universe, Higher Cause, Great Ruler of Events, Supreme Architect of the Universe, Author of the Universe, Great Creator, Director of Human Events, Supreme Ruler, and, very rarely, Fate or Fortune. All in all, Washington's was the language of the Freemasonic Lodge more than of the Christian sanctuary.

The republican fathers took the Deist tenets for granted. Some sort of God held people accountable now or later because morality had been implanted as a possibility in people. The nation being born must be responsible and must seek virtue. No individual sects commanded enough loyalty or breadth to serve as energizers for the whole national community. What each held separately about salvation was of no consequence to the public weal. In this reckoning it seems amazing that these ideas could issue forth in the same colonies that had just been agitated about the Great Awakening, and even more amazing that the same people could show allegiance to both systems of thought.

Washington was not seen as an intellect. He was revered for his piety. Then and ever since the pious have portrayed him uncharacteristically on his knees at Valley Forge. They have forged documents and spread legends that make him sound more orthodox than he was. He went to church with less than reasonable regularity, paid his pew rent, took his long turns as a vestryman, rarely commented about church, was not a regular at the Lord's Supper, and not once in his life was caught saying anything remotely evangelical. But in his Farewell Address and often elsewhere he saw morality and religion to be the twin props of society, depending upon each other.

James Madison is more important as an agent of religious liberty and an enemy of establishment than as a religious philosopher, though he more than most contemporaries fused Enlightenment and evangelical thought, perhaps under the influence of John Witherspoon. Benjamin Franklin was a far more interesting case. Curious about everything including the rhetoric of evangelists, he paid them his respects. But his scientific curiosities led him to found the American Philosophical Society in 1744 and to direct energies more in that direction than to the churches.

Franklin, like Jefferson, accented nature more than reason, experiment more than ideology, morals more than ideas. A fairly orthodox Deist with a Christian reminiscence, he almost puckishly evaded Christian theological affirmations.

I had been religiously educated as a Presbyterian; and tho' some of the dogmas of that persuasion, such as eternal decrees of God, election, reprobation, etc., appeared to me unintelligible, others doubtful, and I early absented myself from the public assemblies of the sect, Sunday being my study day, I never was without some religious principles. I never doubted, for instance, the existence of the Deity; that he made the world, and govern'd it by his Providence; that the most acceptable service of God was the doing good to man; that our souls are immortal; and that all crime will be punished, and virtue rewarded, either here or hereafter. These I esteem'd the essentials of every religion; and, being to be found in all the religions we had in our country, I respected them all, tho' with different degrees of respect, as I found them more or less mix'd with other articles, which without any tendency to inspire, promote, or confirm morality, serv'd principally to divide us, and make us unfriendly to one another. This respect to all, with an opinion that the worst had some good effects, induc'd me to avoid all discourse that might tend to lessen the good opinion another might have of his own religion; and as our province increas'd in people, and new places of worship were continually wanted, and generally erected by voluntary contribution, my mite for such purpose, whatever might be the sect, was never refused.

On the key evangelical point, What think ye of Christ? he waffled. A month before he died he answered Ezra Stiles' specific query on that issue. "I have, with most of the Dissenters in England, some Doubts as to his Divinity; tho' it is a question I do not dogmatize upon, having never studied it, and think it needless to busy myself with it now, when I expect soon an Opportunity of knowing the Truth with less Trouble." But he saw no harm in its being believed if that belief made Jesus's doctrine more respected and better observed—especially since Franklin could not note that "the Supreme" took such an attitude amiss by discriminating against unbelievers with any marks of displeasure.

Jefferson could be more frontal and serious. Timothy Dwight, Calvinist, Orthodox, defender of the faith, Yale President, and Federalist hated Jeffersonianism, as did his New England peers. At century's end John M. Mason in a sermon warned against electing Jefferson president. To Mason, Jefferson was an infidel, an atheist. "Ponder well this paragraph," in which Jefferson said that "The legitimate powers of government... extend to such acts only as are injurious to others. *But it does me no injury for neighbors to say there are twenty Gods or no God. It neither picks my pocket nor breaks my leg.*" Said Mason: "Ten thousand impieties and mischiefs lurk in [that paragraph's] womb." "This is the morality of devils."

In his White House years Jefferson would paste together excerpts from the Gospels, the miracles all having been excised, to show how great are *The Life and Morals of Jesus of Nazareth*. He was a sort of theist, a believer in God, respectful of the non-dogmatic Jesus. He regarded the world as having been created, and he pictured an after life.

Morality was innate. Reason had limits, but nature was an open Bible. Jefferson was a qualified optimist about the future, largely on religious grounds. Yet he also saw corruption and feared for the future. Government had to be limited, because of the temptations of power and its ready abuses. He saw himself as one who transcended sectarianism, but he contributed to a kind of sectarian view of his own over against the other sects.

Just as Edwards had taken a millennial vision to "the whole nation," these defenders of reason and nature in religion constantly stressed the public and social consequence of religious choices. Samuel Adams feared that "our Enemies have made it an Object, to eradicate from the minds of the People in general a Sense of true Religion & Virtue."

Revelation assures us that 'Righteousness exalteth a Nation'—Communities are dealt with in this world by the wise and just Ruler of the Universe. He rewards or punishes them according to their general Character. The diminution of publick Virtue is usually attended with that of publick Happiness, and the public Liberty will not long survive the total Extinction of Morals."

The religion of reasonableness was becoming the religion of the Republic. It was not theologically compatible with evangelicalism, as the militants in both camps knew. But psychologically and politically the two could coexist, and they did. Timothy Dwight wrote an ungainly satirical poem on "The Triumph of Infidelity," in which he pictured present and future horrors of reasonable and republican people prevailing. G. Adolf Koch, historian and friend of *Republican Religion* titled his book's last chapter "The Triumph of Fidelity," because of religious orthodoxy's subsequent victories. Both were right. Both triumphed and have been woven together in the minds and hearts of American citizens and subcommunities and in "the whole nation" or the "communities [that] are dealt with in this World by the wise and just Ruler of the Universe" whom they both acknowledged.

8

Let Us Give This Experiment Fair Play

The Great Awakening and the religious support for rights and Revolution together represented passage over the "hump of transition" to the social covenant that remains to this day. The Revolutionary era is the "hinge" epoch in the development of American Christianity and religion in general. The energies of men and women in the various colonies were summoned. In those moments and movements we have recognized the main themes of the eighteenth century "faith of our fathers."

The period was characterized by what Emile Durkheim calls "effervescence." Effervescences do not last, as Durkheim and the scientific students of religion recognize. Ferments subside, what has been viscous crystallizes, minds open in periods of revolt close when they belong to people who have recently acquired power. Boredom, weariness, exhaustion, reaction, entrenchment all follow. There comes a time when people engage in mopping up operations, when they tie up loose ends. The final decades of the eighteenth century represent such a period of institutionalization.

The attitudinal Revolution that preceded the War of Independence did have to be completed after it. The churches, thrown into upheaval by the War and the shocks of nation-building, had to reconstitute themselves. This period is often looked back upon as a time of radical changes. Drastic alterations there were: from that period came the guarantees of religious freedom, the separation of church and state, and the invention of denominationalism—all breaks with most Christian pasts. They exacted determination and skill from many people. But they were following through on a logic determined between the 1740s and the 1770s. In retrospect, of course, the solutions to problems of that period look automatic as they could not have to the people who saw themselves exploring uncharted territory. But they possessed compasses and landmarks; there were valleys in that terrain within which they had to move and barriers there that they had to avoid.

The great question that remained as the generation of 1776 yielded to that of 1787 was this: What should be done with religion in the Republic? The Declaration of Independence did not yet clearly picture a nation made out of "the United States," even though Abraham Lincoln four score and seven years later helped enshrine the attitude that it did. The conclusion that the colonies that sent delegates to the Continental Congress should become a nation dawned on different advocates at different paces. But by the time of the Constitution the question of whether there would be a nation had receded. The terms of colonials' life together had become urgent, and religion was a nagging issue.

Today it is hard to picure the perplexity that the problem occasioned. One must look to nations in which religious factions have been at war in recent times to understand the outlook of the people of the 1780s. Northern Ireland, India-Pakistan, multi-religious Indonesia, African states where Muslims vie with tribalists and Christians, and Lebanon, are all societies that exemplify something of the substantive matter that faced the colonists. True, the founders were basically dealing with Protestant sects and not with different religions, but neither sixteenth century continental Protestiantism nor seventeenth century England were reassuring examples of how to avoid bloodshed in religious controversy.

In nine of the thirteen states religion was still established in the 1770s. Admittedly many of the official arrangements had been relaxed. Apathy about religion was one of the great aids to concord. The War had helped jostle the colonies toward further adjustments and accommodations. Yet most of these nine colonies did not give indications before the War that they would willingly yield their establishments. The new state constitutions that were written between 1776 and 1784 had made great moves toward general disestablishment. But the idea of one nation with at least two establishments, a Congregational one in the North and an Episcopal one in the south, had to be entertained among people who could not envision alternatives.

The first alternative that came to mind was what is called "multiple establishment." The South Carolina Constitution experimented lightly with this in 1778, and even George Washington pictured it a choice preferable to mere disestablishment. But practical problems would have been immense were this to become a generalized policy. And too many confessors of reasonable and pietist religion had no use for such a solution. Their revolutions had moved too far to permit them to settle for such an unsatisfactory compromise.

Disestablishment was really the only choice, and between the 1770s and 1833 it occurred everywhere. The result was a polity that virtually all Americans endorse and all take for granted. Retrospect helps us here once again. But to the people who had enjoyed establishment the move was threatening. In the long view of Christian history the move *was* epochal. In a notable passage Sidney E. Mead called the change a "momentous revolution in the thinking and practice of Christendom," so radical that even Jefferson could speak of it both in 1782 and 1808 as an "experiment," though a "fair" one. Mead quoted Winfred E. Garrison:

> For more than fourteen hundred years ... it was a universal assumption that the stability of the social order and the safety of the state demanded the religious soli-

darity of all the people in one church. Every responsible thinker, every ecclesiastic, every ruler and statesman who gave the matter any attention, held to this as an axiom. There was no political or social philosophy which did not build upon this assumption... *all*, with no exceptions other than certain disreputable and "subversive" heretics, believed firmly that religious solidarity in the one recognized church was essential to social and political stability.

For this reason Mead could call it one of the "two most profound revolutions which have occurred in the entire history of the church," so far as its administrative side was concerned—the other having been the establishment of Christianity in the Roman Empire early in the fourth century. In other words, the Revolutionary years in America meant the most visible legal assault on Constantinianism, Augustinianism, medievalism, and Christendom that had yet occurred.

Because the change was epochal, momentous, profound, and revolutionary, it is easy for later religious historians to assume that at every turn it demanded radical thought or issued in intense conflict. That was not the case; in most colonies and on the federal level the change was made almost by elision, by slippage and slurring. Even in Virginia and Connecticut or Massachusetts, which left behind a record of some struggles and holding-actions on the part of the old order, the votes were always overwhelming for the new resolutions. And no dead bodies, few imprisonments, and not too many inconveniences resulted—at least if the seventeenth century in American or most of Europe are used as standards for comparison. The nineteenth century historian Philip Schaff "was right," says Winthrop Hudson, "when he asserted that the whole question of religious freedom had been settled prior to the formation of the national government by the previous history of the American colonies."

What made the change easy? The first factor is the growing

precedent in England, which after the Glorious Revolution of 1688 had begun to show tolerance for sects and even to wink at Roman Catholics, who were not to be emancipated until 1829. It was hard for colonials to bear the taunts of England, against whom a Revolution was being waged, to the effect that the colonies were inconsistent in their withholding of liberties on something so basic as religion. The fact that England was surviving while weakening its religious establishment helped breed assurance that government could exist on different terms than those long regarded as the only possible ones.

Precedent in the colonies was a second factor. While Rhode Island had been much despised in the seventeenth century and Pennsylvania and other middle colonies mistrusted in the eighteenth, civil society had continued in them and religion actually prospered there. It was hard to argue against success, even if its character nettled establishmentarians. Add to this the nagging of the sects. It was difficult for an Ezra Stiles or a John Adams to believe that the bare establishments of New England could create scruples for dissenters' consciences. But the dissenters had staying power, eloquence, and the force of example on their side. They became ever more respectable and respected: they had to be listened to. Too many examples of cooperation between churches of both established and disestablished character had developed during the Great Awakening and the Revolution. Should these not be acted upon? Should gained ground be lost?

The reasonable and republican religionists among the founding fathers complemented and then moved beyond these churchly expressions and incidents. Not that all the statesmen were on the side of full liberties for dissent or removal of all privilege from the colonies' official churches. George Washington could live with establishment. Patrick Henry became its last eloquent defender in Virginia. John Adams sided with Boston's elites to hold to special status for

Congregationalism. Even Benjamin Franklin could picture some sort of arrangement whereby dissenters could be happy, and the religion necessary for the masses' morality could be supported.

In James Madison and Thomas Jefferson, however, the new philosophies of nature and reason were fused with legal minds in support of change. Madison may be the most informing example. An Episcopalian who had studied in Scotland and had read Montesquieu and Locke, he also picked up some ideas about religious freedom at Witherspoon's Princeton. While still a young man he railed against "that diabolical, hell-conceived principle of persecution" by which the Virginia establishment lived on and kept power in 1774. "The right of every man is to liberty—not toleration," a distinction lost on the establishment. In 1784 he wrote a "Memorial and Remonstrance" against the Virginia House of Delegates' proposal to assess for the support of the Christian religion. Civil government should not interfere with what Madison believed to be a private affair. He was also concerned about rights of non-Christians, friendly to Jews, and alert to issues that inhibited them or inconvenienced minority Christian groups.

Thomas Jefferson was so proud of his "Bill for Establishing Religious Freedom" in Virginia that he wanted reference made to it on a tombstone that would not even mention the fact that he had been president. Neither the state nor the federal government should give support to religions. This belief did not mark him as an enemy of faith. He even wanted to make provisions for teaching about religion in the University of Virginia, whose founding was the other act he wanted remembered on his memorial stone. Just as Madison had shown that the proper question in the new nation was "not is Religion necessary,—but are Religious Establishments necessary for Religion?" so Jefferson answered it in his *Notes on the State of Virginia* as early as 1782:

Our sister States of Pennsylvania and New York, ...

have long subsisted without any establishment at all. The experiment was new and doubtful when they made it. It has answered beyond conception. They flourish infinitely. Religion is well supported; of various kinds, indeed, but all good enough; all sufficient to preserve peace and order;... Let us too give this experiment fair play...

Between 1776 and 1784 the first State Constitutions were written. In that period every state made some moves for full liberty, within the limits of what they regarded to be public order. For them constitutions were not simply comments on how things were and how liberties could be assured so much as declarations of what government and rights ought to be about. If "We the People" act in concert, we compact with each other; and the people could least readily yield on sacred rights of conscience as they applied to religion. Hence issued the famous "Declaration of Rights" associated with some constitutions. But the time had not yet come in which in every case this momentum could be carried over to disestablishment.

The period after 1784 was the time in which the logic of disestablishment was pursued with intensity. Some citizens were asking whether religion ought not be given support to guide people through a period of threat and uncertainty. In Virginia a Bill of Assessment was proposed as the means of such support; it was against this that James Madison prepared the Memorial and Remonstrance.

Virginia became the scene of decisive struggle. The Church of England, always weak there, was almost destroyed by the Revolution. It lived on under the tutelage of the very kinds of vestrymen who voted at the House of Delegates and who were, in the main, prepared for change. Dissenters were also on the scene. The Regular and Separate Baptists were at the point of linking up. Presbyterians were making noises. Even the quiet Lutherans resented assessments and privilege for Episcopalians. The loosening of establishment ties began in

1776; by 1780 dissenting ministers were legally recognized when they carried out official acts.

Patrick Henry thought this was the moment to strike with a moderate, fair-minded bill that would help churches influence public life. Now the line between civil and religious realms—the line that Jefferson would later solidify into a wall —became visible. Under Madison's guidance the final passage of the Assessment failed and in 1786 Jefferson's "Bill for Establishing Religious Freedom" passed. Almost everyone got what he wanted, except Henry and nineteen other delegates, who lost 76-20. The awakened Christians now had more freedom to move and did not have to compromise on their faith in the face of official and established religions. The statesmen had won the good will of the churches and could count on them to contribute to public order.

Compared to the Virginia intricacies, Georgia, Maryland, and the Carolinas represent relatively uninteresting changes, though it should be noted that some of them still gave second-class status to Roman Catholics and Jews. In Pennsylvania a clause favoring the Old and New Testaments was eventually changed because of Jewish complaints. New York repealed all laws that "may be construed to establish or maintain any particular denomination of Christians." Pennsylvania, New Jersey, and Delaware, of course, had nothing to repeal. Nor did Rhode Island in New England. Vermont came into the union in 1791 with a constitution acceptable on religious issues; it was completed in 1793.

New Hampshire establishment hung on until 1819; the northern drama in Connecticut (1818) and Massachusetts (1831-33) belongs to the nineteenth century. But the heart had gone out of the genial establishments there. The industrious Anson Phelps Stokes almost two centuries later ran a balance sheet on the young states and their consitutions and found widely varied adjustments and no clear pattern beyond general disestablishment. The reckoning deserves mention because it shows that no simple clear ideology had activated the states and no central government could enforce one approach.

Two, Virginia and Rhode Island, conceded full freedom. New York limited freedom only to the point of asking immigrants who were becoming naturalized citizens to abjure religious ties along with all other foreign allegiances. Six "adhered to religious establishment" in wildly different ways. Delaware and Maryland demanded Christianity, while four states required assent to the divine inspiration of the Bible and two to a belief in heaven and hell. In three states ministers could not hold civil offices. Two emphasized belief in one eternal God; Delaware even exacted belief in the Trinity. Protestant clauses survived in five states; South Carolina went no further than to speak of "toleration." Rarely did anyone act upon these vestigial religious exclusions, but they were offensive to minorities. And they suggested a need for the Constitutional Convention to take up the issue.

Surprisingly, religious liberty did not even come up there—a shocking idea to those who make too much of the "separation of church and state" as being central to the young republic. Religion was only mentioned in the Constitution's Article VI: "No religious Test shall ever be required as a Qualification to any Office or public Trust under the United States." That sentence in its splendid isolation serves to "put religion in its place" in more ways than one. But when delegates had to go home and convince their states to adopt and ratify the Constitution, the question kept coming up. Some did not cherish the clause in Article VI. More worried about the absence of a religious clause and of any bill of rights at all. Madison's reassurance that religious freedom "arises from that multiplicity of sects, which pervades America, and which is the best and only security for religious liberty in any society" was strategically reassuring but not legally satisfying.

The silence of the Constitution threw the religious question back to the states; they held this power until the Fourteenth

Amendment in 1863. But the Bill of Rights in 1791 did make some comment on the subject at last, largely because Madison had a change of mind and thought that more should now be said on the subject. "Congress shall make no law respecting an establishment of religion or prohibiting the free exercise thereof." The Constitution itself was and remained metaphysically and religiously non-committal—a fact that has always nettled a minority of Americans who press with little success for a Christian or a religious amendment to the Constitution.

Some of the void left by the decline in official establishment was filled by a millennial language that was current both within and outside the churches. The nation itself would serve as a kind of church, with the support of the churches, to inculcate morality and to be an example to other nations. Ezra Stiles in his famous Connecticut Election Sermon of 1783, *The United States Elevated to Glory and Honor*, prophesized that

> This will be a great, a very great nation, nearly equal to half Europe... Before the millennium the English settlements in America may become more numerous millions than that greatest domain on earth, the Chinese Empire. Should this prove to be a future fact... the Lord shall have made his American Israel high above all nations which he has made—in numbers, and in praise, and in name, and in honor.
>
> I am sensible some will consider these as visionary utopian ideas;
>
> ... How wonderful the revolutions, the events, of Providence! We live in an age of wonders; we have lived an age in a few years; we have seen more wonders accomplished in eight years than are usually unfolded in a century.

Not all was as serene as he suggested. Some did not share the millennial vision and those who did often used it against others. The same New Englanders who had once been

America's Israel against France and then against England now were the chosen people against the Republicans of Virginia and in their own territory. The churches were weak, but their spokesmen held strong visions of the future. Some did see a division of labor: David Austin preached on The *Millennium* in the 1790s:

It seems no unnatural conclusion from ancient prophecy, ... that in order to usher in ... the *latter-day-glory*, TWO GREAT REVOLUTIONS are to take place; the *first* outward and political; the *second* inward and spiritual.

Whether this prophesy was ever to come true or not, Austin was doing what many prophets have done. He was extrapolating into the future on the basis of past events, exaggerating the tendency growing out of them. The clergy had progressively come to believe that two revolutions had already taken place, or at least they had begun. Austin's order had been reversed. The second was outward and political, from the 1760s through the 1790s, while the inward and spiritual revolution had occurred from the 1720s through the 1750s. That was long ago. When Austin spoke the churches had become weak everywhere. Never before or since did a smaller percentage of the American people explicitly identify with churches. But in the midst of that sterile period they, too, were quietly busy institutionalizing themselves in the new republic. Consciously or not—who can tell?—they were preparing for inward and spiritual revolutions to come in the Second Great Awakening and the churching of America in the nineteenth century.

We call this form of institutionalizing "denominationalism," drawing on a word that had begun to have currency in England but which took on new sociological coloration in post-War America. The denomination at times serves clear functions and at others appears to be just as dysfunctional as it is durable. Before the War it was already clear that vast differences separated people within what later were called denominations. New England High Church Episcopalians differed from Virginia's latitudinarians. Old Light fought New Light in Congregationalism; Old Side warred against New Side in Presbyterianism; for a time Regular and Separate Baptists differed. The Awakening and the Revolution created tension and even led to splits within the churches. But another side of each found relatively easy alliances with others.

On those terms, denominations do not protect doctrinal integrity or define their members' creedal positions. Yet they have been designed to do so; they tell something, at least, about belief and identity and purpose. Practically, they work. In the *laissez faire* spirit of nineteenth century business some spokesmen even defended the system as a means of assuring competition and offering a variety of options to the shopper—ideas that had little New Testament warrant or grounding, but that spoke out of and to the American situation. The denomination has even served as a kind of invention to drain off conflict into harmless channels in American life. Denominational warfare can be psychologically vicious, but it rarely disturbs the peace and leaves behind the wounded or dead bodies. Kill a denomination and a new one takes its place. Work for merger and you produce new denominations. Try to be anti-institutional and devise unorganized religion and society organizes a denomination out of the impulse.

Each colonial church or dissenting group, denominationalized after the Revolution and disestablishment, had many adjustments to make. For some the changes were minor. Thus the German-speaking Lutherans and Reformed resumed their church life much as before. They made some moves that drew them closer together, including the founding of Franklin College in Pennsylvania in 1787. The German and, even more, the Dutch Reformed were more acclimatized before the Revolution, and could make alliances also with the Presbyterians and other Calvinists who shared their doctrines.

The Lutherans were theologically more remote from the majority of the Protestants. They were experiencing attrition from several directions. The English-speaking ones had been drifting into Anglicanism for some time. The ecumenical ones formed Union churches with the Reformed. Those in touch with the Continent were often touched by Continental rationalism. Turn of the century hymn books and catechisms of some American Lutherans reflected the mood of Germany's age of reason and were thus out of line with those of the American groups that were prospering. Despite these handicaps, Lutherans showed staying power and, refreshed by new immigrations, were on the way to becoming one of the nation's larger religious groups.

The small German peace sects, the Moravians and Mennonites, the Dunkers and other Brethren, stigmatized for their remembered pacifism, tended to withdraw into ever deeper isolation and never shared in the nineteenth century growth patterns. Quakers did not have linguistic or cultural barriers, but they, too, had lost status for their stance in the War of Independence. Schism and conversions to Anglicanism hurt them. They never recovered momentum and they dwindled.

Ezra Stiles and everyone else's "big three," the more or less established Presbyterians and the old order's embodiments, Congregationalism and Episcopalianism, resumed their central place in the drama, but they had already begun losing relative place among the denominations. The Presbyterians had Princeton as a center, and from it they polished revival techniques. Hence they produced a blend that helped them almost hold their own in the nineteenth century.

Congregationalists made up what was the most potent, literate, exciting, and complex denomination. In the early years of the next century the Old Light Arminians would become Unitarian and form a new denomination. Congregationalism lived with the legacy of pro- and anti-revival factions. Some old orthodox folk lived on to fight all these groups plus the "New Divinity" men, latter-day Edwardseans, who stretched Calvinism as far as they could, generating some of the motivation for the new century's missionary and humanitarian endeavors.

Episcopalianism hardly survived in the South, and one of the first bishops in America surmised that it might die with the death of the "old families." The SPG men, who had been the most energetic, had gone home as Tories. Most of the southern clergy had also left for England. Lay people in the South stayed with the church as part of a way of life, but they did not respond to awakeners. They were on the wrong side in the church-state struggles of the South and too leaderless at first to profit from their more advantageous position as a minority in New England. But they began to face a new century when in 1784 Samuel Seabury was ordained in Scotland; the church finally had a bishop and soon would have two more.

These three churches were to be eclipsed by the Baptists and the Methodists. By 1800 Baptists were strong in all the colonies. They seemed to embody the Great Awakening impulses and served as a means for people to "get religion." They were rural and urban, capable of dealing with the educated (Brown University) and uneducated; Baptists were locally autonomous, mobile. The Methodists had an opposing polity; they were highly controlled, hierarchical, centralized. They suffered for their earlier Loyalism. But Francis Asbury was the right leader for the new day and after 1784 the evangelically Arminian group began its startling climb alongside the Baptists.

In John Carroll, named a bishop in 1784, the Roman Catholics at last found the leader they needed. They were soon to be nagged by Protestant-style issues having to do with the kinds of power lay trustees should have. But within a decade they had a college and a seminary. The French Revolution forced talented priests to seek refuge in America, where they were put to good work. In several decades the new migrants would come to help them find their way as a competitive, purposive, and even evangelistic denomination.

Jews preoccupied themselves with survival and with having Trinitarian and other Christian clauses removed from civil documents. Indians were not free to denominationalize; they were still the objects of missions at best and exiled to reservations or victims of death at the hands of whites at worst. Neither Revolution yet helped them, and the founding fathers for the most part did not entertain an extension of their language of rights into the Indians' worlds. Nor to the Negroes'. Some of the New Divinity men like Samuel Hopkins joined the leftover Quakers in seeking a new way for and toward them. But here again the men of reason, including most notably Thomas Jefferson, compiled no better record than did the most backward sectarians, some of whom spoke out of conscience for the blacks. But by the century's end the blacks began to nurture their own denominations, churches that were to be the prime institutions in Negro life for well over a century. For the most part, Indians and Negroes represented unfinished business and a lack of fulfilment of the promise of American life.

To say that the inner-spiritual and outward-political Revolutions of the eighteenth century provided the landscape in which later American religionists have lived is not to say that their world is reproducible today or that they might recognize their achievements in the forms in which they are encountered today. They were themselves divided, contentious, uncertain. Many of their millennial visions led them to arrogance and pride. Their manifest destiny and mission sometimes destroyed parts of the world they had come to have. God's American Israel had found the promised land, but did not live into all the promise. Some of their language has been traduced beyond recognition; some of their better forms are beyond recall.

Yet the century of Haym Salomon and John Carroll, of Jonathan Edwards and Benjamin Franklin, of Henry Melchior Muhlenberg and John Witherspoon, of George Whitefield and Isaac Backus and Ezra Stiles, of John Woolman and James Madison deserves all the attention it has received. Of such leaders in both Awakened and Republican religion it might be observed just as Forrest Mcdonald has said in closing his book on the formation of the American Republic, *E Pluribus Unum:* "But there were giants in the earth in those days, and they spoke in the name of the nation, and the people followed them. As a result, the Americans were despite themselves doomed forever to be free." The faith of our fathers—and of the nameless but equally talented and devoted mothers—lives still.

References

This reference material has been chosen and described with one purpose in mind: to guide the lay readers into parallel readings should any of them find their curiosity stimulated by the present chapters. By "lay reader" I mean any one in or out of the fields of religion or history who does not specialize in mid-eighteenth century America. The specialists would not use this book as access to primary sources in any case. They would more likely read it as an essay whose interpretations they would compare with their own. Without difficulty they will find their way back to the sources. For all other readers, specific footnoting to such sources is less valuable than is a means of helping them find accessible secondary literature that enlarges upon these themes. I am therefore providing a general essay that leads in general ways to books by other scholars, books in which many references in this book are located and enlarged upon.

I:i. Utmost Good Faith Towards the Indians

In William T. Hagan, *American Indians* (Chicago: The University of Chicago Press, 1961) the reader will find reference to the skull of King Philip, at the beginning of my chapter, and the Declaration of Independence and Northwest Ordinance at the end (pp. 14, 31, 42). The Cotton Mather quotation that opens his *Magnalia* comes from a long excerpt in

Perry Miller and Thomas H. Johnson, *The Puritans* (New York: Harper and Row Torchbooks, 1963), Volume I, p. 163. Other Mather and Edwards quotations come from a discussion in Sidney H. Rooy, *The Theology of Missions in the Puritan Tradition* (Grand Rapids, Michigan: William B. Eerdmans, 1965), pp. 268-70, 294, 299f, while the critical comment of Edwards is in Peter Gay, *A Loss of Mastery* (Berkeley: The University of California Press, 1966), p. 91. The exchange between John Heckewelder and the Indian is preserved as a source in Wilcomb E. Washburn, ed., *The Indian and the White Man* (Garden City, New York: Doubleday, 1964), pp. 111-116.

I: ii. With Equal Force in Favor of the Negroes

Two books will provide elaboration on many themes in this chapter: Winthrop Jordan, *White Over Black* (Chapel Hill, North Carolina: University of North Carolina Press, 1968) and Duncan J. Macleod, *Slavery, Race and the American Revolution* (Cambridge: Cambridge University Press, 1974). For Samuel Sewall, the reference to "separate but equal," and quotations from William Smith, George Berkeley, the Marquis de Barbé-Margois, and John Woolman, see Jordan, pp. 195f., 425, 185, 191, 283f., 273; MacLeod reprints Ebeneezer Hazard, Nathaniel Appleton, and Samuel Hopkins, pp. 17f., and 25.

I: iii. The Jewish Nation or the Infidel Jew

Cotton Mather material comes again from the work by Sidney H. Rooy [see I:i (Whenever a book is being referred to for the second time, the chapter in which it was first cited appears in brackets after the author's name. Thus the reader can trace publishing data.)], p. 247, while Peter Stuyvesant is quoted by Robert St. John in a light and popular history, *Jews, Justice and Judaism* (Garden City, New York: Doubleday, 1969), p. 9.

I; iv. You and All Your Tribes

For the J. Hector St. John Crévecoeur statement see Richard O'Connor, *The German-Americans* (Boston: Little, Brown, 1968), p. 27. Benjamin Franklin is quoted by Jordan [see I:ii],

p. 102. John Tracy Ellis, *American Catholicism* (Chicago: The University of Chicago Press, 1969, Revised Edition), pp. 369 and 374 is the source for the Backhouse words and those by a Philadelphia Jesuit, while Governor Seymour's warning is reproduced by Theodore Maynard in *The Story of American Catholicism* (Garden City, New York: Doubleday, 1960), Volume I, p. 100. See Margaret H. Bacon, *The Quiet Rebels: The Story of the Quakers in America* (New York: Basic Books, 1969) for the words of Samuel Fothergill and William Penn, pp. 63, 49; the second Penn paragraph is in Peter Brock, *Pacifism in the United States* (Princeton: Princeton University Press, 1968), p. 163.

II: i. Neither Soaring too High nor Drooping Too Low

All statistical material or reference to mapping of colonial religion and the location of churches derives from Edwin Scott Gaustad's *Historical Atlas of Religion in America* (New York: Harper and Row, 1962); see Gaustad for the growth of Episcopal churches and for similar data in subsequent chapters. Raymond W. Albright, *A History of the Protestant Episcopal Church* (New York: Macmillan, 1964) is cited on the Great Awakening (p. 24) and is the source for the references to George Keith and Timothy Cutler (pp. 81, 64). The judgment of Episcopalianism is in Daniel J. Boorstin, *The Americans: The Colonial Experience* (New York: Random House; 1958), p. 131 while Hugh Jones is cited on p. 123. There is a reference to the work of Norman Sykes on eighteenth century England; see Norman Sykes, *Church and State in England in the XVIIIth Century* (Cambridge: Cambridge University Press, 1934).

II: ii. Slow to Grasp the Meaning of the American Situation

The best book on Presbyterianism in this period, from which I have taken several summary paragraphs, is Leonard J. Trinterud, *The Forming of an American Tradition* (Philadelphia: Westminster, 1949), pp. 36f.

II: iii. A Terrible Shake unto the Churches of New England

For more on "the heart prepared," see Norman Pettit, *The Heart Prepared: Grace and Conversion in Puritan Spiritual*

Life (New Haven: Yale University Press, 1966). On Solomon Stoddard and The Half-Way Covenant see Robert G. Pope, *The Half-Way Covenant: Church Membership in Puritan New England* (Princeton: Princeton University Press, 1969), pp. 251-57). The Timothy Dwight quotation in Stoddard's critique of ministers appear in James W. Jones, *The Shattered Synthesis: New England Puritanism before the Great Awakening* (New Haven: Yale, 1973), pp. 107, 116f. Edwin Scott Gaustad reproduces Nathanael Emmons' worries, in *The Great Awakening in New England* (New York: Harper and Row, 1957), p. 112. The Cotton Mather section relies in part on Peter Gay, *A Loss of Mastery* (see I;i), pp. 65, 71, 73, 82, 84, 86f. The quotation from the Saybrook Platform is in H. Shelton Smith, Robert T. Handy and Lefferts A. Loetscher, *American Christianity: An Historical Interpretation with Representative Documents* (New York: Scribners, 1960), Volume I, p. 227. For Samuel Willard see Jones; *The Shattered Synthesis*, p. 75

III. The Surprising Work of God

The Henry Scougal and Whitefield quotations are in John Pollock, *George Whitefield and the Great Awakening* (Garden City, New York: Doubleday, 1972), pp. 10f., 12; Pollock's is so novelistic and pious a work that I cannot recommend it, however. For Benjamin Colman and for the best treatment of revivalist tensions in Connecticut, there is C.C. Goen, *Revivalism and Separation in New England, 1740-1800* (New Haven, Connecticut: Yale, 1962), especially p. 104 at this point. On evangelicalism, see Lawrence A. Cremin, *American Education: The Colonial Experience, 1607-1783* (New York: Harper and Row Torchbooks, 1970), p. 313. The first Perry Miller reference is his *Errand into the Wilderness* (Cambridge: Harvard University Press, 1956), p. 155. A number of other comments by Miller and Alan Heimert are taken from the introduction to Alan Heimert and Perry Miller, *The Great Awakening: Documents Illustrating the Crisis and Its Consequences* (Indianapolis: Bobbs-Merrill,

1967), pp. x, xvii, and xiv, and Alan Heimert, *Religion and the American Mind* (Cambridge: Harvard University Press, 1966), p. 10. For William McLoughlin's theoretical summary see his *New England Dissent*, 1630-1833 (Cambridge: Harvard University Press, 1971), Volume I, pp. 329ff. There is also a reference to Jerald C. Brauer's utilization of Eliadean motifs. The reader who cares to see a development of this should consult Jerald C. Brauer, ed., *Reinterpretation in American Church History* (Chicago: The University of Chicago Press, 1968), pp. 1-28.

IV. That Battering Ram Against Our Church

Alexander Garden is quoted by Alan Heimert [see III], pp. 36f. A valuable book on the issues evoked by the possibility of the settlement of an Episcopal bishop is Carl Bridenbaugh, *Mitre and Sceptre* (New York: Oxford University Press, 1962), the source of the quotations from Henry Caner, Timothy Cutler, and, later in this chapter, Ezra Stiles. See pp. 85, 83f., 10f. For reference to Wallace and other important materials on the southern Presbyterians, see Ernest Trice Thompson, *Presbyterians in the South, 1607-1861* (Richmond: John Knox, 1963), Volume I, p. 39; p. 53 reproduces Robinson's words. McLoughlin is quoted from his book on New England Dissent [III], p. 324. Ezra Stiles' first reference here is from Alan Heimert and Perry Miller [III], p. 595, while Charles Chauncy was quoted by James Jones, *The Shattered Synthesis* [II: iii], p. 187.

V. The Revolution of God's Great Design

On Methodism and Pietism, see Alfred North Whitehead, *Adventures of Ideas* (New York: Mentor, 1955), p. 30. For Cutler on Tennent, see Gaustad, *The Great Awakening in New England* [II: iii], p. 33. Chauncy is quoted from James W. Jones [II: iii], pp. 188f. For Edwards' psychological views, see Heimert and Miller [III], pp. xxxix ff. For the discussion of Southern religion, see Samuel S. Hill, Jr., *Southern Churches in Crisis* (New York: Holt, Rinehart and Winston, 1967). The Bushman quotation is in Richard L. Bushman, ed., *The Great*

Awakening: Documents on the Revival of Religion, 1740-1745 (New York: Atheneum, 1970), p. xiii. On laicism and democracy see Goen, [III], pp. 28 and 31. He is also the source of the Increase Mather reference, p. 9. On itinerancy, see Carl Bridenbaugh [IV], p. 51, where the Jonathan Law incident is detailed. The summary comment is from Michael Zuckerman, *Peaceable Kingdoms: New England Towns in the Eighteenth Century* (New York: Knopf, 1970), p. 112n. Gewehr is quoted at length in Anson Phelps Stokes, *Church and State in the United States* (New York: Harper and Brothers, 1950), Volume I, p. 243. The second Gewehr quotation is from Thompson [IV], p. 60. On the millennial character of Edwards' views, see Heimert [III], pp. 64f.

VI. Religion and Public Liberty and Intimately Connected

John Adams' familiar words appear, among other places, in Bernard Bailyn, *The Ideological Origins of the American Revolution* (Cambridge, Massachusetts: The Harvard University Press, 1967), p. 1. Bailyn is also the source of quotations later in this chapter from Isaac Backus, Andrew Eliot, and Jonathan Mayhew; see pp. 263 f., and 256. A number of references are from the forthcoming Yale University Press book by Nathan Orr Hatch, *The Sacred Cause of Liberty: etc.* From his Washington University dissertation we quote Edmund Morgan, p. 8; Jonathan Edwards on the idea of a concert of prayer, p. i; Samuel Davies on the art of war, p. 31, 24; Samuel Adams, p. 61; Joseph Huntington, p. 159; Samuel Sherwood, p. 1. On Loyalists, see William H. Nelson, *The American Tory* (Boston: Beacon, 1964), pp. 89-91. The reference to John Gilmary Shea is in John Tracy Ellis, *Catholics in Colonial America* (Baltimore: Helicon, 1965), p. 400. The story of Catholicism is recounted in Charles Henry Metzger, S.J., *Catholics and the American Revolution* (Chicago: Loyola University Press, 1962); Metzger quotes Jonathan Mayhew on corrupt Rome, p. 10. John Carroll is cited by Maynard [I:iv reference], p. 7. Peter Brock [I:iv] is the source for the quotations from the Philadelphia Yearly Meeting, and Tom Paine; see also Brock's own summary, pp. 186, 190, and 278.

Raymond Albright [II:i] is the source for Seabury's words while the reference to Joseph Galloway is in Edward Frank Humphrey, *Nationalism and Religion in America, 1774-1789* (Boston: Chipman Law, 1924), p. 67. Edmund Burke is cited by Anson Phelps Stokes in *Church and State in the United States* (New York: Harper and Brothers, 1950), Volume I, pp. 277f. For the context of the Hanover Presbytery's statement, see Thompson [IV], Volume I, p. 93. Elias Boudinot is quoted from Trinterud [II:ii], p. 243. William McLoughlin [III], I, 571f., is the source for Backus quotations here. The famous reference from Peter Oliver appears in Alice M. Baldwin, *The New England Clergy and the American Revolution* (New York: Ungar, 1958), p. 155. Charles Chauncy citations are from Heimert [III], pp. 248, 277. Bishop Secker is quoted by Albright in the work cited earlier in this chapter, p. 102. At the end of the chapter are references to Thomas Kuhn's work on paradigms. See David A. Hollinger, "T. S. Kuhn's Theory of Science and Its Implications for History," in *The American Historical Review* (April, 1973), Vol. 78, No. 2, pp. 370ff.

VII. Religion is Divided into Natural and Revealed

A fine historical tracing of natural and republican religion is in Sidney E. Mead, *The Lively Experiment* (New York: Harper and Row, 1963); from it we have quoted Mead himself, pp. 27 and 52f. and, near the end of the chapter, Benjamin Franklin, p. 45. Peter Gay is again quoted on Jonathan Edwards; see *A Loss of Mastery* [I:i], p. 91. On tradition and change, see Michael Hill, *The Religious Order* (New York: Crane, Russak, 1973), p. 2. Conrad Wright is exceptionally good on *The Beginnings of Unitarianism in America* (Boston: Beacon, 1955); from him we quote John Wise, pp. 136f, and Samuel Johnson, p. 19 as well as Cotton Mather, and

Jonathan Edwards a little later, p.9. The sources in John Opie, ed., *Jonathan Edwards and the Enlightenment* (Lexington, Massachusetts: D. C. Heath, 1969) are used here, especially in reference to Perry Miller, pp. 22f., 29, and 35. Jones, *The Shattered Synthesis* [II: iii] provided material from Ebenezer Gay, pp. 132f., 138-142 and Jonathan Mayhew, p. 149. Jonathan Mayhew is quoted by Cedric B. Cowing, *The Great Awakening and the American Revolution: Colonial Thought in the 18th Century* (Chicago: Rand McNally, 1971), p. 200, as well as by G. Adolf Koch, *Religion of the American Enlightenment* (originally titled *Republican Religion*) (New York: Crowell, 1968), pp. 196, 201f. Ezra Stiles' words also appear in Koch, pp. 16f. as do those of Charles Chauncy, p. 193 and John M. Mason, pp. 270f. The lengthy excerpt from Franklin is in Stokes [VI], Volume I, p. 294. On Washington's names for God, see Paul F. Boller, Jr., *George Washington and Religion* (Dallas, Texas: Southern Methodist University Press, 1963), pp. 94ff. For Samuel Adams see Clinton Rossiter, *The Political Thought of the American Revolution* (New York: Harcourt Brace and World, 1963), pp. 204f.

VIII. Let Us Give This Experiment Fair Play

The Sidney Mead summary and the passage by Winfred E. Garrison appear in Mead, *The Lively Experiment* [VII], p. 60. See Winthrop Hudson on Philip Schaff, in Hudson's *Religion in America* (New York: Scribners, 1973, Revised Edition), p. 99. For Madison, see Stokes [VI], pp. 304ff. Jefferson is quoted from Sidney Mead, p. 60. For Stiles see Hudson pp. 109f. Austin is quoted in Hatch [VI], p. 149. The closing quotation is from Forrest McDonald, *The Formation of the American Republic 1776-1790*, originally titled *E Pluribus Unum* (Baltimore: Penguin, 1965), p. 236.